CREATING
~ THE ~
PEACEFUL
HOME

CREATING

∽ THE ∽

PEACEFUL

HOME

Design Ideas for a
Soothing Sanctuary

ANN ROONEY HEUER

MetroBooks

MetroBooks

An Imprint of the Michael Friedman Publishing Group, Inc.

First MetroBooks edition 2002

©1999 by Michael Friedman Publishing Group, Inc.

Library of Congress Cataloging-in-Publication Data Available Upon Request.

ISBN 1-58663-595-6

Editor: Reka Simonsen
Art Director: Jeff Batzli
Designer: Stephanie Bart-Horvath
Photography Editor: Wendy Missan
Production Manager: Camille Lee

Color separations by Colourscan Co Pte Ltd
Printed in Singapore by KHL Printing Co Pte Ltd

1 3 5 7 9 10 8 6 4 2

For bulk purchases and special sales, please contact:
Michael Friedman Publishing Group, Inc.
Attention: Sales Department
230 Fifth Avenue
New York, NY 10001
212/685-6610   FAX 212/685-3916

Visit our website:
www.metrobooks.com

DEDICATION

For my cherished family circle: Fred, Marlene, Elizabeth, Francis, Ellen, and all my other treasured friends and relations. For Reka Simonsen, my insightful editor at Michael Friedman Publishing. And for my late friend, celebrated author Dr. Leo Buscaglia, who reminded us all to "live in love" to create a world of kindness, compassion, and peace.

CONTENTS

INTRODUCTION   8

Chapter One
UNDERSTANDING THE GENTLE POWER OF PLACEMENT
      AND DESIGN   18

Chapter Two
CREATING SANCTUARIES WITH COLOR   40

Chapter Three
MIRRORING NATURE THROUGH TEXTURE AND PATTERN   62

Chapter Four
RELAXING WITH SOOTHING FURNISHINGS AND ACCESSORIES   78

Chapter Five
PERSONALIZING YOUR ROOMS WITH SACRED TREASURES   96

Chapter Six
ENHANCING TRANQUILITY WITH LIGHTING, SOUND,   110
      AND FRAGRANCE

Chapter Seven
DISCOVERING PARADISE: OUTDOOR LIVING SPACES   126
      AND GENTLE GARDENS

SELECTED BIBLIOGRAPHY   142

INDEX   143

INTRODUCTION

"Our house . . . had a heart and a soul . . . it was of us, and we were in its confidence and lived in its grace and in the peace of its benedictions."

—Mark Twain

When do our houses become our homes? Does it happen in an instant, when we sign closing papers, or does our passion for our houses grow stronger over time, as we celebrate birthdays and holidays in them, plant gardens, watch our children play, and spend weekends adding on or fixing up? Just as it takes years for an acquaintance to become a cherished friend, so too does it take time for us to feel a deep affection for our houses. It happens slowly but surely, when we allow the beauty of our spirit to spill over into our living spaces.

OPPOSITE: Tall, frosted windows with dramatic black frames and sashing bring plenty of natural light into this elegant, understated living room. The neutral color scheme and minimal furnishings enhance the sense of tranquility in the space.

In classic films and books, we often discover that the most fascinating houses have distinct personalities, shaped by the peaceful or malevolent people that abide in them. In the movie *Gone With the Wind*, Tara was a welcoming Southern mansion, dearly loved by the gracious O'Hara family. However, in Daphne du Maurier's mystery *Rebecca*, the gray stone mansion by the sea, Manderley, was anything but genteel. The lingering presence of its dead mistress made it cold and sinister.

In real life, you never know the truth about a house until you've stepped inside its front door. A house may be exquisitely built and perfectly decorated, but if it doesn't mirror the characters of the people that live within its walls, it's merely a showpiece without a soul. Yet if a house reflects the passions of its owners, and if it embraces family and friends alike with comforting sights, fragrances, sounds, and textures, it becomes a sanctuary from the world outside—and it truly feels like a peaceful home.

Throughout history, countless writers have rhapsodized about the romance of home and hearth. Nineteenth-century American poet John Howard Payne wrote, "Be it ever so humble, there's no place like home." Payne's contemporary, English poet Robert Southey, said, "There is magic in that little word, home." The author who wrote perhaps most engagingly on the subject, however, was the American Mark Twain. To him, home was a spiritual, sympathetic presence.

In the 1870s, Twain envisioned a mansion that would provide not only a place for luxurious entertaining, but also a comforting refuge for him, his wife, and their three daughters. Twain hired a prominent New York architect, Edward Tuckerman Potter, to build his nineteen-room dream house in picturesque Hartford, Connecticut. The end result was a grand Victorian confection of polychrome brickwork accented with

LEFT: To keep in step with nature, alter the accessories of your favorite rooms to reflect the changing seasons. Here, a cozy living room celebrates summer with the addition of sunny pillows and flowers and a filmy drapery that invites in the sunlight.

OPPOSITE: The rapture of sunlight, a woodsy view, and a cozy fire make this living room irresistibly appealing. The room's earth-toned furnishings and pottery, as well as the stone fireplace and geometrically sashed windows, pay homage to the Arts and Crafts style.

gingerbread ornamentation, turrets, and gables. This mansion was home to the Twain family from 1874 through the early 1890s, and among its more memorable rooms were a glass-enclosed conservatory with a sparkling fountain and a red billiard room with a hexagonal balcony that reminded visitors of a Mississippi steamboat. The design and decor of the house reflected the extravagance intrinsic to the Victorian period and Twain's eccentric, humorous nature.

Despite Twain's love for Gilded Age opulence, the room that was likely his sanctuary had a quiet ambience born of muted jewel tones and rich textures. It was the master bedroom, designed for slumber and creative reflection. The

focal point of the bedroom was a luxurious black double bed that had been created an ocean away in Venice, Italy. The story goes that Twain and his wife, Olivia, would often lie at the foot of their "bedstead" so that they could admire the masterfully carved cherubs atop the twisted columns of its headboard. Perhaps these gentle angels inspired Twain, for it was from his bed that he dictated his autobiography and was photographed while working on storylines for such literary classics as *The Adventures of Huckleberry Finn*, *The Prince and the Pauper*, and *A Connecticut Yankee in King Arthur's Court*.

As the Twains discovered in their Victorian retreat, a sense of peace can be found when a home feels like a kindred spirit, offering us safe harbor from the world outside our doors. It doesn't matter if the house is huge or small, vintage or contemporary, grounded in the city or rooted in the country. What is important is that we truly live in it, and transform it from a functional shell into a private paradise.

In centuries past, the very idea of designing a home for privacy and refuge from the clamor of society was unheard of. According to architect Witold Rybczynski, author of *Home: A Short History of an Idea*, in

fourteenth-century France, the poor lived in crowded one-room hovels while the merchant class lived in bourgeois town houses, which served as both workplaces and shelters. One main room became a shop or work-room for conducting business, while a large hall was used for preparing meals, eating, entertaining, and communal sleeping. Furnishings had several purposes—collapsible beds doubled as seats, and tables could be used for bedding down if guests stayed overnight. By the seventeenth century, however, single-family houses were being built in such countries as France, England, the Netherlands, and Germany for businessmen who

wanted a separate residence away from their commercial enterprises. And by the eighteenth century, privacy and luxury had become paramount to the European bourgeois. Comfortable furnishings and specialized rooms designed solely for sleeping, dressing, entertaining, dining, or cooking were now fashionable.

The lighting in our homes directly affects our physical and emotional comfort level. This room's plentiful sunlight and lush view create a naturally warm and friendly environment for entertaining or for such hobbies as painting or quilting.

CULTURAL TRADITIONS OF PEACE IN THE HOME

Through the ages, certain cultures have bestowed a mystical sense of peace upon their homes through their spiritual connections to nature. When Columbus came to the New World in 1492, historians estimate that there were approximately fifteen million native Americans in North America. Depending upon their tribal ways, their shelters were either temporary or permanent, and were made of earth, willow, reeds, bark, wood, stone, straw, animal hide, or other natural materials. Hivelike pueblos in the Southwest were built from clusters of adobe brick or stone, while portable tepees were made of bark or animal hides and designed to open up to the rising sun. Inside the homes were the necessities of life, such as food and cooking utensils, hunting tools, religious objects, backrests made of willow, warm buffalo robes, personal belongings, and little else.

To native Americans, home with its circle of fire traditionally has been a holy place. Mother Earth is a divine source of materials, tools, and beauty, and the Great Spirit speaks through river and sea, forest and hill, buffalo and salmon, gentle winds and fierce thunderstorms, and, indeed, all creation. In the late 1800s, Susan LaFlesche Picotte, the first native American woman to become a physician, declared, "The home is the foundation of all things for the Indians." Her sentiment is echoed in the Omaha Indian tribal chant, "Remember, remember the sacredness of things. . . running streams and dwellings, the young within the nest, a hearth for sacred fire."

While native Americans believe that all human life is intertwined with nature, the ancient Japanese people believed that natural objects such as rocks, trees, waterfalls, streams, and mountains were the dwelling places of *kami*, or spirits. The spiritual paths of Shinto (the indigenous religion of Japan) and Zen Buddhism continue to inspire a strong affinity for the outdoors among the Japanese; in fact, the people perceive their homes and gardens as one harmonious entity without boundary.

Japanese interior design respectfully celebrates the splendor of the four seasons through such items as delicate paintings, colorful screens and banners, and translucent sliding doors that open onto nature. Also, the home or garden tea house is the center for the tea ceremony, often described as the heart of Japan's traditional culture. Introduced to Japan by Zen monks in the twelfth century, the tea ceremony is an intricately orchestrated ritual designed to spotlight beauty and hospitality and to inspire a serene state of mind. The ceremony invites appreciation for simple pleasures: enjoying artfully prepared tea and cakes, admiring perfectly arranged flowers, caressing cherished old pottery, sitting on tatami mats made of woven rice straw, and sharing quiet reflection among friends. While crowded conditions make compact apartments and homes the norm in modern Japan, the Japanese devotion to cleanliness, order, nature, and ancient traditions leads them to create intimate and calm living spaces.

Today, we read much about the ancient Chinese art of *feng shui* (pronounced "fung shway") in relation to the harmony of our homes, offices, and gardens. Feng shui, which means "wind" and "water," offers us specific ways to select appropriate sites for building our dwellings and to arrange our interiors to create optimum environments for happiness, creativity, growth, health, and success. Feng shui suggests that everything in the universe is represented by five elements: Water, Fire, Earth, Wood, and Metal. The natural environments in which we live can be classified by their main element; for example, if you live in an English country cottage surrounded by a garden and trees, yours is a Wood environment.

Our office and home interiors are also ruled according to their primary element; for example, an office featuring steel storage cabinets and a window that overlooks a river spanned by a metal bridge has a Metal landscape.

While our interior environments are a mosaic of all five elements, if one element overpowers the others, there is imbalance. For example, an unruly garden that reminds us of the overgrown thicket around Sleeping Beauty's castle has far too much Wood element, and needs to be pruned in order for us to feel in control. Another aspect of feng shui

is the concept of *chi* (or ch'i): cosmic energy. Chi is all around us and, according to Taoism, the ancient religion of China, it is either "yang" (lively, positive, bright) or "yin" (calm, reflective, soothingly dark). The complementary forces of yang and yin must be in balance for us to know a sense of serenity. If we spend the day at the beach, actively collecting seashells and building sand castles, we experience good yang energy. But if we're Christmas shopping in a crowded department store with few clerks and long lines of customers, we'd likely be frustrated by excessive yang. When we take a bath by candle-light, we soak in a velvety atmosphere of soothing yin. Yet if we spend our weekdays deprived of natural light in a dismal office cubicle, we experience the dark side of yin.

LEFT: Impressionist painter Claude Monet once said, "More than anything, I must have flowers, always, always." Inside and around the home, flowers add ephemeral beauty and provide emotional solace.

OPPOSITE: A gentle place for rest or meditation, this traditional Japanese bedroom embraces natural colors and patterns through its tatami mat, blue and white cotton futon cover (*futonji*), and the lovely woodwork and translucent paper of the shoji.

Inside our homes, if our rooms are overburdened with too much yin or yang, they make us feel uncomfortable. An abundance of yang contributes to crowded and littered spaces, while too much yin creates a negative, hostile, even deathly ambience. We know there is imbalance if our rooms feel too cluttered or bright, or too gloomy or chilly. The key is to allow chi to flow through our rooms—in one entrance and out another, like shafts of sunlight that stream through the living room window to the floor and down the hallway. Many things can influence the movement of this energy, including color, shape, texture, fragrances, sounds, icons, running water, and wind chimes. Removing obstacles that block the flow of chi (such as large or badly placed pieces of furniture) is said to bring harmony and balance to our rooms and our lives.

CREATING YOUR OWN PEACEFUL HOME

The very fact that we're contemplating how to make our homes more personally fulfilling shows that we are ready to begin a journey of the spirit and the senses. It is time for us to think deeply about what we see, hear, smell, touch, and taste in our favorite living spaces, both indoors and out. Does each room enchant and calm? Or is there too much chaos in one or more of our rooms due to a lack of space, inadequate lighting, blaring televisions or CD players, or a host of other annoyances?

Chances are good that your home, like mine, is a wonderful "work in progress" that is filled with memories—and possibilities. Although our houses have evolved into highly efficient machines for fulfilling our physical needs, we also want them to be spiritual beacons in the storm. Home should always feel like a loving place that we can escape to, a place that makes us feel renewed like an idyllic mountain retreat or the summer cottages of our childhood. Now, more than ever, it seems that we need "time out" from the frantic pace of the technological age.

Millions of us spend more than forty hours a week at the office, but even when we're away from our desks, work often intrudes on our private lives. Office e-mails and voice mails, cell phones and pagers can bring vital information to us day and night—but they can also disturb our sense of home as a haven from the demands of our jobs. After spending our days inside airtight office buildings and then navigating through heavy traffic, we're understandably tired. But when we get home and turn on the television, we often see disturbing news reports of wars, starvation, homelessness, natural disaster, and local tragedy.

Since its unveiling at the New York World's Fair in 1939, television has entertained and enriched us with great performances, natural wonders, and award-winning educational programs that have sparked our children's zest for reading and learning. Still, it plays too prominent a role in many homes. In the United States alone, the average television set is on for more than seven hours a day. Not surprisingly, by the time most children graduate from high school, they will have spent fifty-four percent more time in front of a TV than in the classroom. That's an alarming statistic, considering that on average, prime time programs feature five acts of violence per hour, not to mention over twenty acts of violence in one hour of cartoons. Psychologists believe that repeated exposure to media violence is responsible for the increased aggressiveness and desensitization of our children.

Fortunately, we can turn off offensive TV programs, log off the Internet, and disconnect the telephone when we choose. But we can't walk away from the demands of our work schedules and the myriad needs of children, aging parents, friends, schools, places of worship, and communities. One magazine article after another suggests that what adults crave is quiet time to enjoy family and home. It makes sense, then, to slow down and celebrate them. Physicians say that chronic stress can weaken our immune systems, leaving us vulnerable to infections and the threat of such illnesses as heart disease, high blood pressure, ulcers, and depression. We should listen to our doctors—and to our hearts.

Our homes should be sacred places that remind us of humanity's eternal connections to trees and sky, oceans and streams, rocks and flowers. They should be serene havens where we can enjoy comfort and technology while staying in tune with the stars, the winds, and the cycle of the seasons. As we look around our homes, there are fond memories in the paintings and photographs, stories in our beloved furniture and accessories, and enchantment in our colors, textures, patterns, and the gentle flow of our rooms. The air is a balm to our souls, for it's scented with fragrant flowers, perfumed candles, or, perhaps, freshly baked pies or bread. Sunlight washes each room with a radiant glow. Our rooms aren't perfect, for homes are meant to be lived in; yet they reflect that which we find lovely and calming, and awaken us to the sensory pleasures all around us.

Since chronic stress can make you vulnerable to serious illness, it's wise to spend some time each day relaxing and rejuvenating yourself in a natural environment. This kitchen harmonizes with the outdoors through gentle colors and wooden beams, an expansive view of trees, and cheerful cattails placed on either side of the sink.

Within the pages of this book, you will visit tranquil indoor and outdoor living spaces, including master bedrooms and meditation altars, light-filled living rooms and spirited kitchens, serene bathrooms and ornamental gardens, all offering a feast of decorating ideas. You'll discover that even simple changes can have a significant impact—such as rearranging furniture for better balance and flow, paring down large collections, rethinking window treatments to invite more light in, and introducing accessories from nature, such as bouquets of fresh-cut flowers, lush potted plants, and trickling fountains.

Before making changes to your home, it's wise to sit down with your family and brainstorm about what might contribute to a more soothing, comforting home environment. Talk about how you live in each of your rooms, how they make you feel, and what furnishings, accessories, colors, textures, and patterns might contribute to their gentle

ambience. While a living room is the perfect social gathering spot for family and friends, a forgotten attic or a screened-in back porch might become your private domain for reading, letter writing, or painting far-off landscapes. Once you share your expectations and ideas, you can begin to renew your entire home or simply change one room to create a blissful sanctuary.

The journey you will take is one of mindfulness, paying attention not only to the material comforts that bring you peace, but to the heartfelt words and treasured family moments that make your house a home every day. Nobel Prize–winning author Albert Schweitzer said that our souls suffer if we live "superficially." By searching deeply for the beauty and blessings of our lives and by celebrating the people we love in countless words and deeds, we have each begun to create a peaceful home, a place— and a feeling—that will remain in our hearts forever.

UNDERSTANDING THE GENTLE POWER OF PLACEMENT AND DESIGN

"An interior is the natural projection of the soul."

—Coco Chanel

In a very real sense, your home has both an outer and an inner landscape. The dance of the seasons, the weather, and the sun alter the way your house and gardens appear from one hour to the next. Your interior landscape changes most noticeably, however, according to your visions and desires, not nature's cycles. It's exciting to think that you have the power to create rooms that mirror your passions and evoke a sense of serenity. Yet where do you begin to look for inspiration?

OPPOSITE: A striking fireplace of smooth, carved wood and rugged stone sets the tone for a nature-inspired living room that is both elegant and warm. Soft furnishings in earthy hues, a sisal rug in a herringbone pattern, and botanical artwork are the perfect finishing touches.

Some interior designers suggest a simple yet effective solution: create a "beautiful home" file to help you picture the home of your dreams. Anything that inspires you can be included—photos from decorating magazines, ads for furniture and appliances, postcards, strips of gift wrap, paint samples, fabric swatches, travel and art gallery brochures, snapshots of summer cottages from your childhood, and so on. As simple as it sounds, undertaking such an exercise can help you discover what design styles, furnishings, colors, textures, patterns, and places speak to you of tranquility. After you decide what kinds of furnishings and accessories you'd like to use in a particular room, try another easy project. Make a rough drawing of your room, indicating permanent features such as doors, windows, and closets. Then cut out small paper templates to scale for each piece of

OPPOSITE: This neutral-hued kitchen is alive with pattern and texture. The contrast of the steel hood and pendant light with the unobtrusive wooden cabinets and floor, as well as the rough, woven chairs with the smooth, upholstered chairs, creates visual and tactile excitement. The subtle color scheme is highlighted by vivid flowers and fruits.

LEFT: How walls are finished can significantly impact a room's perceived proportions and overall mood. This cottage bedroom seems refreshingly light and spacious because of its soft honey-hued wall-paper and white ceiling, as well as its neutral bed linens and carpeting.

furniture to visualize possible room arrangements. This may sound like child's play, but it can give you concrete ideas when renewing a room.

The process of transforming your home into a peaceful haven starts with keen observation. First, look at the "bones" of your rooms: the windows, walls, floors, ceilings, staircases, doorways, and any other architectural structures. Consider the traffic patterns of each room in light of where furniture, appliances, and built-in features are placed. Finally, look at each room as a whole. Does every element seem to fit, or is something in the mix visually or emotionally jarring? What is it about each room that

you like and what is it that you'd consider changing? Remember that just as people can juggle several roles each day, so can the rooms we live in. A seldom-used dining room might be transformed into a part-time library, entertainment center, or home office. A bedroom corner can be used for creative pursuits such as sewing, sculpting, or painting watercolors.

The first two things to consider when planning to design or rejuvenate a room are proportion and balance. If you've ever seen yourself in a carnival funhouse mirror, then you know how silly a tiny head looks on top of an unnaturally large body. The same disproportionate effect occurs

ABOVE: The spirit of this elegant living room is serene and inviting. Gentle neutral colors, contrasting textures, soft lighting, cozy furniture groupings, and fragrant flowers all help to create a warm sense of welcome.

OPPOSITE: A deep devotion to the splendor of the seasons is a hallmark of the Japanese home. The neutral palette of this living room forms a lovely backdrop for the room's thriving plants and the expansive windowed wall.

if a miniature vase is used for the centerpiece on a huge farmhouse kitchen table or if a small chair is placed next to a sprawling sofa. The visual weight of the items doesn't work because one overpowers the other. Visual weight isn't just related to size and shape, however. Warm and vivid colors and brightly illuminated rooms have more visual weight than cool, muted hues and dimly lit living spaces, for example. In interior

design, proportion requires furnishings to be selected and arranged so that they create a sense of balance and harmony. A room appears to be balanced when its blend of similar and contrasting colors, textures, patterns, furnishings, and accessories create a symphony of beauty, with no one element outshining the others.

There are several tried and true ways to create a sense of balance in your rooms. The more elegant and traditional styles of decor often rely on symmetry. If your living room's focal point is a bay window positioned in the center of a wall, imagine that the room has been divided in half by an invisible thread. Decorate each side of the bay window with a loveseat, end table, and lamp, and you create formal symmetry. You needn't choose identical furnishings or objects, but the pieces you use should be similarly sized and shaped to give the illusion of mirror images.

Asymmetrical arrangements are more free-spirited and casual. Let's say the focal point of your family room is a white stucco fireplace. If you group a romantic French Provincial chair and small painted trunk on one side of the fireplace, you can balance it with a larger French Provincial settee on the other side. Radial balance, on the other hand, radiates out from a central point in a room. For example, if your sunroom's focal point is a centrally located fountain, all the furniture and plants should be positioned an equal distance from the fountain and from one another, like spokes on a wheel.

This Japanese-inspired living room is a tranquil still life of delicate hues, contemporary furniture, and plants placed to evoke thoughts of *wa*, nature's harmony. The delicate carving in the doorway and the assorted traditional fabrics add color and a sense of history to the room.

Serene Decors: A Japanese Living Room and Dining Room

In Japan, interiors are furnished and decorated with an eye toward simplicity, proportion, and balance. A typical Japanese living room might be furnished with two beige sofas and two matching armchairs, a hibachi (a portable fireplace with a deep hollow to contain the fire) converted into a coffee table, two colorful ceramic hibachis used as planters, and a *tansu* (a freestanding chest used for display). The heavier sofas and armchairs could be arranged in a symmetrical U formation in the center of the room, while the lighter hibachi planters could flank the ends of the U. In the middle of the U would be the hibachi coffee table. As long as this table spans no more than two-thirds of the length of each sofa, it will sufficiently anchor and balance the furniture arrangement. Against a wall at the other end of the living room would be the tall tansu decorated with plants and Japanese porcelain. By placing this large item in opposition to the sofas and chairs, the arrangement helps balance the visual weight of all the furnishings in the room.

In a traditional Japanese dining room, the focal point of the room is often a long, rectangular *kotatsu* table, centered in the room atop tatami matting. The table might be graced with a single porcelain bowl or teapot for accent and color. On the long sides of the table, in place of chairs, would be floor cushions positioned for seating. Each wall would be sparsely decorated with one lovely banner, and sliding shoji screens would allow gentle light to radiate throughout the room. This picture is one of symmetry, elegant simplicity, and balance, with every element in proportion to its surroundings.

LEFT: This symmetrically balanced corner enchants with a mix of contemporary furnishings, neutral hues, and gleaming woods and metals, all designed to provide a calm space around the room's glowing fireplace.

OPPOSITE: From the Industrial Age to the Information Age, Arts and Crafts style has endured because it celebrates nature and skilled handwork, as well as simple yet elegant designs, rich textures, and jewel colors. Arts and Crafts hallmarks in this dining room include the floral-patterned rug, the rich woodwork and cabinets, and the ornate window design.

Designs for Peaceful Living

Along with proportion and balance, several other factors affect the physical and emotional harmony that you feel throughout your home. Color, texture, pattern, furnishings, accessories, window and floor treatments, lighting, sound, and fragrance all come into play in creating the memorable sanctuaries you count on for quiet reflection or relaxing with family and friends.

The design philosophy of innovative German architect and International style furniture designer Ludwig Mies van der Rohe (1886–1969) was "Less is more." His doctrine underscores our longing for simple, peaceful, nature-inspired home interiors. Throughout this book, we'll highlight six soothing decor styles (Arts and Crafts, Cottage, Eclectic, Japanese, Minimalist, and Southwestern) that echo Mies van der Rohe's beliefs, celebrating pared-down beauty, comfort, and natural materials, patterns, and accessories.

Arts and Crafts   Today's Arts and Crafts interiors take their inspiration from two late-nineteenth-century movements: the English Arts and Crafts movement led by poet and designer William Morris, and the American Arts and Crafts movement heralded by furniture makers Gustav Stickley,

Elbert Hubbard, Charles Limbert, and others. The Arts and Crafts philosophy was best described by Morris: "Have nothing in your houses which you do not know to be useful or believe to be beautiful." This guiding principle is reflected in the Arts and Crafts emphasis on craftsmanship, and on colors and patterns inspired by fruits, flowers, foliage, birds, and, indeed, all of nature.

In reaction to cluttered Victorian interiors, the poorly made factory furnishings of the Industrial Revolution, and the harsh new synthetic (aniline) dyes of the era, William Morris established a factory in 1861 to produce furniture, stained glass, tiles, fabric, and wallpaper. His products emphasized honest design, skill, and craftsmanship. Morris and his followers looked to the craft guilds of the Middle Ages for inspiration and advocated that each craftsman should be an artist. Some of the key elements of timeless Arts and Crafts decor include simple wooden furnishings (especially upright, rectilinear, unembellished oak); muted jewel-colored fabrics and wallpapers sporting Morris-style flora and fauna motifs; pillows featuring homespun fabric and embroidered medieval designs; lanterns and furniture hardware of bronze or hammered copper; stained- and leaded-glass windows; art pottery; glazed tile or stone fireplaces; handmade rugs; and simple wrought-iron or copper candle holders.

Cottage   The cozy lure of the seaside, lakeside, or mountain cottage appeals to our desire to escape the impersonal technological age. Cottage living has been popular since the nineteenth century, when families with means spent summers away from sweltering, polluted cities in the restorative air of the countryside. Cottages are generally small, compact dwellings,

and that is part of their enduring charm. In times past, the colorful glass panels over the doorways of cottages often sported the Latin motto *Parva sed Apta*—"small but just right."

Cottage interiors often have tongue-and-groove paneling painted white, cream, butter yellow, Swedish gray-blue, or other pastel or neutral hues. Furnishings are often wicker, wood with distressed paint, or simple upholstered pieces in neutral hues topped with bright or pastel pillows in toile, plaid, ticking, gingham, or chintz. Wooden plank floors are left bare or topped with neutral-colored mats, Oriental rugs, or vivid hand-hooked rugs. Cottages often feature cobblestone or wooden fireplaces, and windows are left bare or dressed with simple curtains.

Decorative accents in the cottage reflect a love of traditional handicrafts and an appreciation of nature's bounty. Lace can appear almost anywhere: at the windows, on tables and dressers, over the backs of chairs and sofas, and above four-poster beds. Vintage quilts are collected and put to use, as are antique colored-glass bottles and ironstone or enamelware pitchers, which are filled with garden flowers. Garden ornaments are often used for accent indoors, and radiant window boxes, planters full of posies, and soothing, rhythmic rockers reside on the porch.

Eclectic   Eclectic design has a broad appeal because it allows you to mix elements of several decorating styles to create your own unique look. If you love the curvaceous walnut chairs and armoires of French country as well as the sleek look of contemporary metal and glass coffee tables, you can combine the two if you carefully orchestrate your room's basic elements of design, keeping in mind such considerations as form, scale, color, and texture. The eclectic approach allows your rooms to be more personal than

This light, airy bedroom successfully mixes furnishings and details from several styles. French antiques, such as the handsome barometer on the mantel, are juxtaposed with the clean lines and pale hues of contemporary furnishings. The monochromatic color scheme is accented with the fresh green of potted plants and the vibrant hues of garden-fresh poppies.

ABOVE: What an ideal spot for curling up with a good book or watching the inhabitants of the nearby woods. The focal point of this private sanctuary is the enchanting forest view that can be seen from all three sides of the alcove.

OPPOSITE: The free-spirited design of this sunroom helps make it a welcoming place for both conversation and solitary relaxation. Despite the room's soaring ceiling, there is a feeling of coziness, which is enhanced by the abundant natural light, the circle of furnishings, the blend of neutral and warm hues and patterns, and a few cherished accessories from vacations abroad.

predictable, and less formal and potentially rigid than traditional settings. While creating a room that reflects one period is gratifying, so, too, is blending heirloom furnishings, artwork, and assorted accessories that echo different times and places. An eclectic room might mix modern furnishings with classical accessories or perhaps country pieces with folk art from various cultures.

An easy way to create harmony in the eclectic setting is through a monochromatic color scheme, accented with colorful quilts, pillows, paintings, or pottery. In an eclectic dining room, for example, the walls, carpet, and a variety of chair styles might all be done in cream. Or imagine a formal Colonial-style living

Sparsely decorated yet serene, this spacious, Zen-like bedroom is a quiet refuge from the outside world. The room's calm neutral colors, warm woods, filtered sunlight, and playful shadows make it a stress-free sanctuary.

32

PEACEFUL PLEASURES

Clutter-free Spaces

Most families have mounds of "stuff," ranging from years of tax returns and ancient recipe clippings to children's artwork, cherished toys, old clothes, a plethora of tools, and "can't part with it" collectibles. Here are a few old and new storage ideas that can help you find a place for all your belongings, adding to your home's clean, clutter-free ambience and your peace of mind:

- Clear plastic stacking bins with lids
- Rafia storage boxes, colorful hat boxes, or stacked Shaker boxes
- Wire baskets
- Wicker, metal, or plastic mini-chests
- Wall-mounted shelving, hooks, and hangers
- Hanging wardrobes for out-of-season clothing
- Filing cabinets for your important papers
- Colorful ceramic crocks for mail and loose change
- Baskets and crates for toys, shoes, and sports equipment
- Shoe cubby/bench for mudroom or hallway seating and shoe storage
- Modular systems of glazed and closed cabinets
- Versatile bookcases, sideboards, wardrobes, tallboys, entertainment units, kitchen dressers, and hoosier cabinets

The Japanese-inspired home is a place for unadorned natural materials and treasured objects. This room features simple wooden furnishings, a delicate temple lantern, and translucent shoji sliding doors, which filter light and add a sense of serenity.

room with several blue upholstered sofas and chairs, cherry tables, and pewter lamps and candle holders. This blue-themed setting can look intriguing with such eclectic accents as an antique Japanese room screen and a few blue-and-white Chinese porcelain urns displayed on the fireplace mantel.

Japanese   Ever mindful of sacred traditions and beauty, the Japanese are devoted to the delicate artistry of their native furnishings and accessories. Despite their modern lifestyles, they make room in their homes for at least one traditionally decorated tatami room for quiet reflection, which contains a series of natural straw tatami mats and uncluttered furnishings. While visitors may find Western-style sofas, chairs, and beds in many Japanese homes, they will also see proud reminders of the country's craftsmanship and notice the timeless simplicity of Japanese decor. The mood of the Japanese interior is one of calm repose, with an emphasis on natural light and earthy textures, including wood, straw, and bamboo, as well as various neutral and brightly colored textiles such as silk and linen.

You can create a gentle Japanese ambience in your home with a few well-chosen items. Wooden or ceramic hibachi braziers are perfectly suited to serve as coffee tables, end tables, display boxes or planters, and wooden kotatsu tables—once used as warming seats positioned over hibachis—can be used as coffee tables, plant stands, or footrests. Lacquerware is uniquely Japanese, and such items as stacking boxes, standing screens, kimono boxes, and serving trays add elegance to any room. Carved wooden masks from the traditional Noh theater, designed to display various emotions, can create a dramatic mood. Cotton or silk kimonos and paper fans or festive kites add color and texture to walls.

Long silk or linen curtains are ideal for creating simple doorways, as are translucent paper and wood shoji, which softly diffuse light. Shoji are used as window shutters and standing screens as well. Screens—which are also made from bamboo, rush, and painted paper or silk—can decoratively separate areas of a room from the flow of traffic or hide unfinished crafts or paperwork from sight as needed.

Minimalist   In fashion, as in decorating, you can sometimes have too much of a good thing. Consider the elaborate millinery "confections" of feathers, flowers, ribbons, and butterflies that women wore during the Gilded Age, and picture the ornately furnished interiors of their Victorian homes. The late interior designer Billy Baldwin advocated "undecorating" our homes so that we can we can add to our living spaces over time, always making room for delightful new details that reflect our changing interests. If you are devoted to the minimalist style, you favor rooms that embrace you with their straightforward, unfettered spaciousness and breathability.

Minimalism calls for clean lines and handsome, understated furnishings. Natural light is favored, so curtains or blinds should be streamlined and windows left bare if there is an entrancing view. Neutral colors such as white, beige, taupe, and cream are preferred. Accessories are few and carefully chosen, such as a tall, angular crystal vase full of tulips or irises. Wooden floors can be topped with striped cotton or neutral-colored rugs, and pale- and medium-hued wooden furnishings add a sense of tactile luxury. Contemporary tables, lamps, candlesticks, clocks, and vases are often crafted of gleaming metal, adding to the sense of airiness.

Southwestern   The Southwest style is a passionate melange of Spanish, native American, and Mexican influences that dates back several centuries. The thick exterior walls are made of adobe and covered with stucco that is painted white or beige. The ceilings have visible wooden supports called *vigas* (beams) and *latillas* (cedar poles), and often skylights are built in to entice more natural light into the home. Outer windows are traditionally small, while those that overlook interior courtyards or gardens are large. Floors are of natural materials such as flagstone, brick, tile, or pine planks. *Nichos*—small nooks recessed into the walls—display religious icons, books, and collections. Adobe fireplaces are often built into corners, and doorways are often arched.

Furnishings are rough-hewn and show the touch of the artisan: wooden beds, tables, and even doors are decorated with elaborate cut-outs; chests and chairs are painted with colorful folk art motifs; and benches, tables, and chairs are made from pierced leather. Decorative accents are bright and full of ethnic flavor. Mexican tiles, Pueblo pottery, woven Navajo rugs and New Mexican blankets, and other local handicrafts are favored. Native American artifacts such as kachina dolls (which represent Hopi and Zuni spirits) and ceremonial drums are blended with religious icons and folk art pieces to create a spiritually eclectic home. Favored interior colors of Southwest decor include white, beige, terra-cotta, red, gold, pumpkin, chocolate brown, sage green, and Taos blue (think muted turquoise).

Your Private Hideaway

If your walls resound with children's giggles and games, your teenager's pulsating music, or an older parent's cranked-up radio talk shows, chances are good that you long for a little peace and quiet. No doubt most of your rooms are beehives of activity and shared pastimes, and you wouldn't have it any other way. Still, adults as well as children need private sanctuaries for daydreams and passionate pursuits. With a little creativity, your bedroom or bathtub needn't be the only place you can disappear to for a blissful hour of reading and quiet repose. You can still carve out a special haven for yourself. Yet if you're short on space, where do you begin?

First, think about the less prominent areas of your home. Perhaps there's an unused corner in a hallway that's ideal for a romantic table for two for private talks or writing in your journal. Maybe there's a walk-in closet in a guest room that could be transformed into a hobby center. Perhaps, like me, when you were little you loved to spend hours reading and bird-watching by your bedroom window. You can revel in such pleasures again, simply by finding a scenic window in a quiet bedroom, stairway landing, or maybe your living room, and adding a windowseat with storage space inside. This not only provides cozy seating but offers a place to stash extra blankets, books, and photo albums. Other places that can serve as an ideal sanctuary include attics, enclosed porches, sunrooms, garden sheds, and corners of great rooms, family rooms, home offices, laundry rooms, and kitchens. Even the alcove under a large traditional staircase may serve as a pleasant nook for a writing desk and chair. Such a space would also be inviting for reading; simply furnish it

A sense of earth and sky prevails in this eclectic, airy dining room. The sturdy stone floor, Southwestern rug, fresh blooms, and gleaming wood ground the contemporary space with texture and color, while radiant sunlight streams down, adding celestial drama.

Referred to in the nineteenth century as "pictures made of light," vintage photographs capture visions of simpler times. Here, a sepia-toned print blends beautifully with a halo of salvaged architectural pieces and a sofa covered in fabric that resembles a photogram (a simple photographic process that results in strong, graphic designs such as botanical silhouettes).

with a small table, a good lamp, and a cozy chair. If you already have a home office, you may want to soften this space with a squashy chair for after-hours reading, or a daybed or chaise longue for catnaps.

To claim a corner of your living room, family room, or bedroom, you may want to partition it off with a freestanding screen. There's a wide variety of screens available today, and some contemporary styles even invite you to display photos or paintings in their "windows." It's also possible to create a customized room divider from several hinged antique doors, vintage art glass or fiberglass panels, or old painted window shutters. Large armoires or bookcases and tall plants can also act as partitions, and furnishings can be arranged in groupings so that a busy room has different seating and activity areas for family chats, games, snacks, or solitary reading or reflection. For a more fluid room partition, you can buy or make a curtain that matches your wall color and hang it on a decorative rod to section off your private corner from the rest of the room. Very large living rooms, family rooms, or bedrooms can even be cut in two with a modular wall system. This provides an attractive wall made of plywood and glass that is easy to assemble and disassemble as needed.

The furnishings that will add comfort and personality to your private sanctuary depend on your activities: an ergonomic chair, spacious work table or desk, unobtrusive storage area for supplies, and good task lighting are must-haves for hobbyists. Gardeners, of course, need spaces with plenty of sunlight and water, fresh air, casual furnishings, sturdy floors, and adequate counter and storage space. If you don't have a garden shed, a corner of your garage, mud room, or laundry room may be just the space you need to start seedlings and nurture container gardens. And if your heart's desire is to find a quiet corner that makes you feel renewed after a hard day, you may want to furnish a family room, hallway, or bedroom nook with a comfy chair or two, a soft carpet, and a small table or trunk topped with scented candles and fresh flowers. The ambience can be even more enchanting with dimmer-controlled lighting, and the sound of wind chimes or gentle instrumental music.

PEACEFUL PLEASURES

Making Small Rooms Appear Larger

The power of illusion can make a small room appear more spacious and serene. Here are a few simple decorating tips that can help suggest more living space:

- Pale, neutral, or cool-colored wall and window treatments can make rooms look airy and spacious.
- Wallpaper with a multi-dimensional design or a small design (a trellis or small leaf pattern, for example) will make the walls appear farther away.
- A dark wall (think midnight blue or hunter green) that serves as a backdrop for pale molding, furnishings, lamps, and so on will appear to be in the distant background, as the light-colored objects advance.
- Several lighting fixtures will eliminate shadows and brighten the room's mood and dimensions.

- A large mirror should ideally reflect a breathtaking outdoor view, a lovely painting, or the glow of candlelit sconces to make it appear that there is more space beyond the mirror.
- By draping a pretty window with a lace or gauze swag, the natural view itself becomes the far-away focal point, stretching the boundaries of the room.
- For architectural interest, fill a wall with several tall bookcases or entertainment units. These provide additional storage space and a focal point, and give the illusion of a larger room.

CREATING SANCTUARIES WITH COLOR

"The purest and most thoughtful minds
are those which love colour the most."

—John Ruskin

Because color is considered to be the most powerful decorating tool, it is vital to understand how it magically transforms your rooms.

It's incredible to think that the human eye can recognize up to ten million different colors—and that there are unlimited palettes of paint

colors, furnishings, and accessories on the market today. Still, the options needn't seem overwhelming. By remembering a few simple principles,

you can feel comfortable and confident about using the hues you're drawn to.

OPPOSITE: Because blue and orange are complementary colors, the marriage of an orange-gold wall and an azure canvas is inspired.
The rough textures of the handmade pottery, the gnarled branch, and the fireplace mantel contrast beautifully with the elegant carving
and smooth finish of the chair.

The classic design concept of "less is more" is stunningly illustrated in this eclectic living room. Carefully chosen new and antique accessories, cozy earth-toned furnishings and vibrant pillows, and a fireplace surrounded by rich woodwork and marble create a heavenly retreat.

42

A plethora of interior design choices begin with the color wheel—an artist's tool that features primary, secondary, tertiary, and complementary colors. Red, blue, and yellow are the three pure primary colors from which all other hues are derived. Secondary colors are formed when two primary hues are combined: green is made from yellow and blue, orange from yellow and red, and violet from red and blue. Tertiary colors are created when a primary color merges with the secondary color that it lies next to on the color wheel: blue-violet, red-violet, red-orange, yellow-orange, yellow-green, and blue-green. Complementary colors are those that are opposite each other on the color wheel: blue and orange, red and green, and yellow and violet. These opposites make striking duets because warm hues (red, yellow, orange) and cool ones (blue, green, violet) seem more vibrant in one another's company. Two other important color terms to understand are tint and shade. Mixing a color with white creates a tint.

Equal amounts of each will make a strong color (think bright pink), while more white and less color results in a pastel (such as pale rose). Shades are formed when you blend black with a color; examples include midnight blue, hunter green, eggplant, and wine.

It's wise to consider what kinds of natural and artifical light brighten your rooms, because both influence the moods of your colors. If a room

In the home office, colorful paintings and knickknacks, as well as comfortable furnishings and adequate lighting, can help create a mood of ease and efficiency. This casual home office benefits not only from overhead and task lighting, but from abundant natural light, fresh air, and an inspiring garden view.

features a sunlit, southern exposure, you may want to cool it down with a refreshing palette of neutral hues or blues, greens, or violets. North-facing rooms generally receive a more subtle light, so warm colors such as reds, oranges, and golds can introduce a cheerful coziness. Generally, east-facing rooms will receive intense morning sun, while those facing west receive ample sunlight throughout the day. Because rooms with eastern or western exposure experience glare, neutral paint colors are often recommended, since their blended hues work well under various lighting conditions.

Be aware that in paint or furniture stores, where fluorescent lights are usually corrected to resemble daylight, a certain color of paint or upholstery may seem perfect, but at home you may discover that the color looks washed out. If your light fixtures use halogen bulbs, you'll benefit from a clean, white light that produces little color alteration. However, if you have standard fluorescent lights, your hues may appear cooler and bluish, while incandescent lights may add a warm yellow glow to your colors. This is why

The neutral walls, sisal matting, and gauzy sage green curtains play supporting roles while vibrant primary colors take center stage in this living room. These bright hues create a cheerful mood that's echoed by the room's floral bouquet and festive mirror.

More than half the earth's surface is covered by oceans and there are infinite shades of blue in the sky, so it's not surprising that blue reminds us of nature's endless, tranquil horizons. This serene living room is ideal for relaxing, thanks to the peaceful view, elegant furnishings, and lovely interplay of teal walls and a cobalt blue painting with the cream-colored window frames.

experts recommend a trial period before you buy. If you're investing in drapery, upholstered furniture, carpeting, or new paint, first take home samples of each. Hang the drapery or upholstery swatch next to your window. Put the carpet remnant on the floor. And instead of counting on a tiny paint chip to help determine the mood of your walls, invest in a small can of the paint color you're considering and cover a piece of white plasterboard or posterboard with it. Prop this large paint sample near a window in the room you plan to redecorate so that you can see the color in natural and artificial light throughout the day and evening. These simple steps will help you decide whether a certain shade, tint, or pure color creates the ambience you envision.

When landscaping around your home, a rainbow of garden colors can look spectacular. When planning a peaceful inner landscape, however, designers recommend decorating a room with a palette of no more than two or three principal colors, with splashes of accent hues as desired. If you prefer a soothing monochromatic palette of one main color,

you can add visual interest by introducing various tones of the color, complemented by a variety of textures and by touches of a neutral hue such as ivory. Generally, if the colors you select are light, they'll appear to advance, while darker hues will seem to recede. Blue objects will look farther away, but realize that reds will seem closer than they actually are. The advancing and receding qualities of color can help you create welcome illusions, suggesting more space in a small room, or making a large room seem more intimate. Whatever your redecorating project, remember to be true to yourself, and choose hues that delight you.

Stephanie Cattarin, owner of Gallery II, an interior design firm in Buffalo, New York, explains, "Color, as everyone knows, is very subjective. Color theorists will tell you that light, earthy hues such as tan, sage, and sand are peaceful, and they are if you're that type of person. But if your idea of a peaceful evening at home is having ten family members stop in for a throw-together dinner, then red might be the color that makes you happy, calm, and secure."

RELAXING NEUTRAL COLORS

Traditional neutral colors are white, cream, gray, and black, among others. These visually soothing shades are often referred to as "noncolors." Today, a neutral can be any color that is subtle enough to mix with other hues while serving as a supporting player rather than the star. Examples of contemporary neutral colors include butter yellow, gray green, and Swedish gray-blue. Neutral colors are ideally suited for relaxing monochromatic interiors, since such rooms are free of demanding, distracting colors and patterns.

OPPOSITE: The warm ambience of this contemporary living room comes from gently filtered sunlight, neutral sand and seashell colors, and a few favorite books and knickknacks. A bouquet of flowers and a small indoor plot of growing grass bring freshness and life to the neutral palette.

ABOVE: A variety of muted warm and cool hues provides spice in this contemporary living room. The golden tones of the carpeting and beige furnishings are enlivened by accent pillows, a treasured landscape painting, and a unique use of color on the walls by the fireplace.

This Southwestern-style living room charms with its ocher chair and muted jade wall, desert-sand carpet and dark woodwork, fragile golden blooms, and strong iron candlesticks. The turquoise glass bowl cleverly complements the hues of the chair and flowers.

PEACEFUL PLEASURES

Transforming Rooms with Paint

One of the easiest, most inexpensive ways to give a room a serene personality is to repaint the walls in a hue that makes you feel calm and relaxed. Keep these tips in mind when changing the aura of your favorite rooms:

- Soft, pale colors create spacious, tranquil settings; dark hues can suggest coziness.
- Slightly grayed or muddied colors create a look of antiqued elegance.
- To blur the proportions of a room, use the same paint color on the walls, ceiling, and, if you like, the floor.
- If your ceiling is too high, a dark matte paint will bring it down to earth.
- Lift a low ceiling by painting it with matte white, pale blue, or a tint that's lighter than the rest of the walls.
- Washable semigloss and gloss paints are practical choices for highly trafficked rooms such as kitchens, hallways, and bathrooms.

- Gloss paint reflects light, adding a sense of spaciousness to small rooms.
- If your walls have cracks or other imperfections, textured paint can cover the problem areas.
- High-quality paints generally use more pigment than less expensive paints; the extra pigment creates beautiful colors that subtly change with your room's natural lighting.
- For soothing white rooms, select white paint with a warm tint such as beige, pink, or yellow. These tints create coziness, while pure white paint can appear blue and icy.
- Vibrant woodstains (red, blue, green, and the like) can heighten the beauty of natural wood grain in floors and furnishings.

To keep a neutral room visually intriguing, fill the room with a variety of smooth and rough textures, highlighted by light, medium, and contrasting dark-toned furnishings. Paintings, carpets, pillows, and pottery can provide splashes of strong color, adding surprise and interest. Neutral hues also make great partners in rooms with dominant warm or cool hues; just picture a lovely red and white kitchen, a blue and beige family room, or a yellow and cream bedroom.

White   Timeless and flexible, white is perceived as a clean, refreshing, elegant, energizing, and spiritual color. It provides a simple canvaslike backdrop for romantic caresses of other colors, and it charms with a variety of textures, such as wicker, lace, gauzy cotton, chenille, and painted wood. In many Western cultures, white is a symbol of purity and weddings, while in ancient Rome and modern China, white is the color of mourning.

Cream   This versatile color works in every decor, from classical to country. It speaks of antiquity and elegance, and its warmth makes it the perfect partner to deep greens, blues, browns, or black. Cream creates a rich monochromatic setting, and it's also effective as a link to more vibrant colors. It was extremely popular throughout the eighteenth century, when it was used to offset gilded details, and during the Art Deco era of the 1920s and 1930s, when it was a foil for such hues as orange, lime green, and turquoise.

Gray   This chameleonlike color can be either cool or warm. Bluish grays are sophisticated and stately, while pinkish grays are calm and inviting. Gray works well with bright green, light blue, rose pink, and lavender. Silvery gray is traditionally associated with wealth and influence.

OPPOSITE: The ivory and white walls and fireplace of this cozy living room provide a classic canvas for a contrasting blend of mocha, ebony, and oatmeal-hued furnishings and accessories. The dark and light palette creates visual drama and proves that a neutral decor needn't be dull.

Black   Black is a dramatic, classic neutral component of any decorating scheme. It can suggest elegance, sophistication, authority, strength, independence, or, in many Western cultures, mourning. Black and white are a timeless interior design and fashion duet, as are black and yellow and black and red. In India, the colors black, yellow, and red have been historically perceived as protectors against jealous, evil spirits.

QUIET, COOL COLORS

For the last six decades, color studies in the United States, Canada, and western Europe have found that considerably more than half the adults polled named blue as their favorite hue. Those who didn't choose blue selected green, or, to a lesser extent, red or white. What this tells us is that a large majority of adults are drawn to cool colors for personal, emotional, and cultural reasons. Since cool colors are calming and relaxing, it's not surprising that we gravitate toward them. Throughout the home, cool hues encourage slowing down, daydreaming, and unwinding from busy days. Quiet spaces such as bedrooms, bathrooms, sitting rooms, romantic dining rooms, and beckoning porches—along with rooms shimmering with sunshine—are ideal stages for palettes of cool blues, greens, and violets. By accenting a dominant cool hue with one or two warm colors

such as terra-cotta, ruby, or buttercup, a cool room will evoke a sense of welcome, and never a chilly "blue mood."

Blue   The mystical color of sea and sky, blue has been revered the world over as a regal, tranquil hue. To Christians, Hindus, and Hebrews, blue suggests spirituality, while to the Japanese, blue has traditionally symbolized spring and victory. An extremely versatile color, blue can dominate a cool scheme, creating a refreshing contrast to white, for example, or it can play a supporting role in a decor filled with bright or muted yellows or reds. Available in a wide range of hues from robin's egg to Wedgwood and indigo, blue's personality can be either formal or casual, and it evokes a comfortable and serene mood.

Green Perceived as a holy color in Muslim countries, green is said to be the most restful color to look at, because its light rays fall most directly on the retina. A symbol of growth, long life, and rebirth, green is associated with concentration and reflection. It refreshes, lends balance, and inspires emotional growth. One of the pleasures of decorating with this hue is that you can mix and match several different greens, such as emerald green, olive, and gray green, and they'll blend into a harmonious garden, just as they do in nature.

In this eclectic living room, the cream-colored walls are warmed by an array of deep-toned wood, teal and midnight blue furnishings, and an impressive assortment of books and collectibles. Note how the flowers and fruits create an intimate feeling despite the grand scale of the room.

PEACEFUL PLEASURES

Nourishing Body and Soul in the Kitchen

As the heart of your home, your kitchen is truly a living room that family and friends gravitate to for good food, conversation, and company. Enhance your kitchen's embracing ambience by providing nourishment for the five senses, from taste to touch.

◉ Create an appetizing visual feast by choosing a variety of warm and cool colors for your cabinets, countertops, furnishings, appliances, dishes, hand-painted tiles, tablecloths, fresh fruits, and flowers.

◉ Draw the eye to an elegant focal point in the kitchen: graceful cabinetry with detailed moldings, a special finish, or glass front doors; an antique kitchen dresser showcasing a few cherished pieces of china or family photos; a lovely old-fashioned fireplace; a vivid stained-glass window.

◉ Invite tactile and visual exploration through a variety of textures, such as cool stainless steel sinks and warm wooden cabinetry, gleaming copper pans and a nubby woven tablecloth, or velvety roses and waxy tulips from the garden.

◉ To emphasize comfort over efficiency, hide kitchen appliances behind louvered doors or in special units. Or, if your appliances wear a soft neutral shade, they can melt into the background while more vivid furnishings or accessories attract attention.

◉ Evocative, delicious scents (and samples) of fresh baked bread, hot mulled cider, and homemade soup entice everyone into the kitchen. Other welcome kitchen scents that can calm and cheer include fragrant candles, fresh flowers, and potpourri made from citrus peel and spices.

◉ Give mealtime a relaxing outdoor ambience by playing CDs featuring nature's music (the soothing sound of bird calls, waterfalls, gentle rain, or the sea) blended with classical music.

Violet Violet or purple, like the color blue, has been a symbol of aristocracy and religion through the ages. Long ago, it was favored by Japanese nobility, Roman emperors, and other rulers for stunning robes that indicated power and affluence. When used in the home, purple is said to represent comfort and spirituality, encouraging introspection and creating an air of mystery. Often, lighter shades of purple such as lavender are used on expansive walls and upholstery to suggest a dreamy calm, while deeper, more dramatic purples are counted on as accent

In this neutral-hued bedroom hideaway, a rich mélange of wood tones and the sensual textures of filmy cotton and decadent silk provide a lovely setting for romance and rejuvenation. Note how the ornate mirror, antique headboard, soft lighting, and vivacious pink blossoms and bedspread add warmth and a sense of luxury.

colors. Deep purple is not recommended for large areas or reflective surfaces, however, because this hue produces a yellow afterimage. Also, deep purple can be associated with mourning.

Just as gazing at a field of blue flowers is said to help slow the pulse rate, spending time in a restful blue room also can be good for body and soul. This lovely cottage bedroom charms with its hand-painted chair and screen dressed in cornflower blue and moss green stripes. The sheer draperies and terrace garden add to the room's tranquility.

A blue-gray wall acts as a cloudlike backdrop for a small contemporary sink, simple mirror, and marine bulkhead–style light fixture in this understated bath. The painted wall has the subtle, translucent quality of a watercolor, which creates an intriguing sense of light and space in the room.

57

WARM, HEALING COLORS

Just as sunshine is tonic to your body and spirit, so, too, are rooms decorated with such cozy hues as red, orange, or yellow. These bright colors are exhuberant, passionate, and never shy. They welcome, cheer, and create a romantic sense of intimacy. Warm hues, in fact, are perfect for social rooms such as dining rooms, kitchens, family rooms, great rooms, and children's rooms. Such vivid palettes are fitting for north-facing rooms, which receive cool, limited light. They're also ideal for spaces with few or no windows and for rooms used for nighttime entertaining. For example, dining rooms have traditionally been done in red because when illuminated by candles and incandescent lights, red walls and draperies reflect the light and create an intense firelight glow.

Red   One of the strongest colors of the spectrum, we associate red with royalty, love, passion, courage, drama, and high energy, as well as with war, fire, blood, and anger. A pure red color scheme can be overpowering, so many designers opt to use it as an accent. Softer reds such as raspberry, terra-cotta, magenta, or deep rose can serve well as a room's major color. Red is said to speed up the body's metabolism and prolonged exposure to it is thought to increase the flow of adrenaline. Often used in restaurant decors, red is also believed to stimulate appetites and promote sparkling conversation.

Yellow   The healing color of the sun, yellow was perceived as a royal hue by emperors in ancient China and by France's "Sun King," Louis XIV.

Through the ages, yellow has also symbolized spiritual and intellectual enlightenment. We associate yellow with good cheer, hospitality, and energy, and admire its beauty in such everyday jewels as daffodils, sunflowers, lemons, and fields of golden wheat. In home interiors, yellow suffuses our rooms with light and can provide a glowing contrast for dark furnishings and accessories. Yellow-toned paint, fabrics, and lighting can make a room seem to smile and can inspire creativity. When you combine bright or muted yellows with a blue, red, green, white, lavender, or gray that has a similar depth of color, you can create a warm and welcoming kitchen, dining room, home office, or bedroom. Yellow is especially well-suited for kitchens, where gleaming pots and pans and shiny enameled fixtures heighten its appeal.

Orange   A daringly bold hue, orange is associated with cheerfulness, conviviality, stimulated appetites, warning, and safety. When we think of orange, we picture our morning juice, tangerines, apricots, mangoes, pumpkins, and roadside tiger lilies and California poppies. Soft orange tints such as apricot, peach, or coral are often used in dining rooms, entry halls, and kitchens and for expansive walls, draperies, and upholstered chairs. These cheerful colors create a warm welcome, stimulate the appetite and the senses, and are conducive to hospitality.

A fresh coat of paint can energize or tranquilize a room. Warmer hues, such as the deep salmon that brightens these walls, are often chosen to inspire sparkling conversation and hearty appetites in dining room and kitchen settings.

SERENE DECORS:
A SOUTHWESTERN KITCHEN
AND FAMILY ROOM

When we think of Southwestern decor, the line between the outdoors and the indoors is blurred. The sunbaked hues of cactus and desert sand, the cooling tones of rugged mountains and canyons, and the sorbet-colored sunsets are all invited inside to recreate the mystical, sacred beauty of earth and sky.

In a typical Southwestern-style home, neutral, warm, and cool colors are powerful tools that evoke the wild frontier beauty of Arizona, New Mexico, Southern California, and Texas. The kitchen might feature ivory-hued modern appliances coexisting happily with ancient-looking white stuccoed walls, exposed ceiling beams, and rich, dark wooden cabinets. Hand-painted, decorative Talavera tiles would add visions of birds and flowers or geometric shapes to a central work island or breakfast bar, the sink backsplash, and the room's focal point, a venerable fireplace. Crafted in Puebla, Mexico, Talavera tiles offer a variety of cool and warm colors, rich glazes, and delightful Moorish designs. The kitchen's warm floor of terra-cotta tiles and dark wooden farmhouse table, chairs, and massive carved armoire, as well as curvaceous hanging iron pot rack and rustic wrought-iron chandelier, add a sense of time-lessness. The colors of a red-orange, turquoise, gold, and black Navajo rug are echoed in the woven pillows on each chair at the kitchen table. The table setting also mirrors the room's warm and cool hues, with a white pitcher full of wildflowers, turquoise wine glasses, and white dishes with a blue, black, and red-orange design.

In the home's family room, the Southwestern color palette of muted, earthy hues reigns supreme. The room's focal point is an unadorned picture window, which frames a spectacular vista of rolling mountains and smooth desert. The surrounding stucco walls are painted a soft hue such as peach, and the floor features terra-cotta tiles from Mexico. Several beige loveseats topped with pillows in rich browns and ochers are gathered around a white fireplace with stepped adobe shelves built into the wall. On the shelves sit colorful native American and Hispanic pottery and carved animals. An antique carved wooden bench resides on one side of the room, while an old wooden table painted a muted turquoise graces a corner, displaying a basket of red, orange, and yellow flowers that mirror the room's warm Oriental carpet. Lush green plants in baskets and terra-cotta pots also add cool color, shape, and texture to the sunlit room.

This living room is an oasis of comfort and peace with a contemporary Southwestern flair. The rich glow of a copper-faced fireplace recessed in a subtly textured wall is the focal point of a room that generates warmth through its glowing embers and candles, its palette of warm colors and natural textures, and its sunny lakeside view.

CHAPTER THREE

MIRRORING NATURE THROUGH TEXTURE AND PATTERN

"Nature has a healing power."

—Diane Ackerman

As astounding as it sounds, it's been estimated that most women and men in the United States spend about eighty-four percent of their lives indoors!

Common sense tells us that anytime that we can stroll along shady forest paths, relax by a lake, or plant a garden must be beneficial. Robert Ornstein,

Ph.D., and David Sobel, M.D., coauthors of *Healthy Pleasures*, are advocates of the restorative powers of nature. They believe people should devote time

every day to deliberately looking at and appreciating the natural world. Inside the home, they suggest, "A peaceful reverie, decreased blood pressure, and

stress reduction may be no further away than an aquarium, the smoldering embers of a fire, or a picture of a waterfall."

This kitchen is a treasure trove of smooth and rough textures. The sleek steel cabinets contrast dramatically with the rugged stone wall.
Fresh flowers and glossy, colorful pottery add to the visual and tactile allure of the room.

In today's high-tech, fast-paced world, we hunger to connect with nature. It happens in unexpected moments, when we watch a dazzling summertime lightning show, listen to the honking of migrating geese in autumn, feel soothed by the lullaby of howling winter winds outside our snug bedroom windows, or smell the intoxicating fragrance of the first springtime lilacs. Without doubt, these spiritual blessings add pleasure to our daily routines—and they help us remember that nature, and the sense of wonder it inspires, isn't reserved for children. It's something we can enjoy every day in our homes, both indoors and out.

Color, of course, is a wonderful way to mirror the beauty of sea and sky, forest and field, canyon and desert throughout our homes. But color never stands alone. It's accompanied by two other surface elements, texture and pattern, that help awaken our senses. Everything in our homes has texture, from the smooth patina of a polished wooden floor to the rough texture of a coir doormat.

RIGHT: This sunlit family room is filled with a lush variety of colors, textures, and patterns. The rugged stone fireplace with its sleek marble mantel, as well as the polished woodwork, deep-pile carpeting, and comfortable furnishings, create a neutral counterpoint to the bright array of warm- and cool-colored throw pillows and the sky blue crystal dish on the table.

OPPOSITE: This warm, eclectic kitchen beckons with a variety of textures ranging from sleek metals and woods to rough straw and dried flowers. The warmth of the room's antique farmhouse table and tangerine walls is complemented by the cool bayberry green of the fireplace and trim.

Textures are generally described as either shiny or smooth, or rough or matte. Shiny or smooth textures such as glass, metal, marble, gloss paint, and silky fabrics can make a room seem brighter or larger, because they reflect light. Such surfaces are useful in kitchens and other activity areas; an overabundance of reflective surfaces, however, can create a cold, clinical ambience. Rough textures that remind us readily of nature, such as wooden ceiling beams, rustic furniture, stone and brick floors, and sisal carpeting, or soft velvet pillows and artfully arranged pussy willows, for example, absorb light and sound, and suggest a cozy ambience. By

contrasting smooth and rough, and shiny and matte textures, we can enjoy the exciting visual and tactile juxtaposition of manufactured and natural materials. We can also observe the fascinating interplay of light upon texture, which can heighten or subdue a color scheme.

As a general rule, designers suggest keeping scale in mind when designing with pattern. Large patterns look fitting on expansive walls, floors, and window treatments, while small patterns are just right for small surfaces. Bold designs, like vivid colors, will advance and make a room appear smaller, while subtle patterns and colors will retreat into the background and make a space appear larger. While some designers feel a room should feature no more than two or three different fabric motifs, others believe you can successfully blend up to ten fabric patterns as long as they harmonize. This is achieved when the patterns incorporate a similar color or colors, exude the same formal or casual ambience (for example, both silk and velvet are elegant), and feature designs of various scale. Identical patterns in several different color schemes (called colorways) or patterns that are very similar and share the same palette also can create interest without causing discord. Interior designers agree that the patterns in a room's wallpaper, upholstery, curtains, and rugs are vitally important; the treatment of such large areas impacts the room's overall mood.

The place for sunny breakfasts and candlelit dinners, this dining room harmonizes with nature through its antique wooden shutters and bleached floor, the delicate lace tablecloth with botanical motifs, the lush floral centerpiece, and, of course, the unrestrained views of earth and sky.

Some Nature-inspired Products for Your Decor

Since your rooms are places where you nurture your family and yourself, they should reflect the tranquil getaways or seasons of the year that delight you. No matter what earthly paradise stirs your soul, the look and feel of many nature-inspired home products can connect you to the wilderness. Here are a few timeless ideas.

Flooring Options   Wood floors offer durability, excellent insulation, and unbeatable aesthetic appeal. Created from such trees as oak, maple, birch, pecan, pine, redwood, and beech, wood flooring styles include solid strips; unit blocks in brickwork (staggered planks), herringbone, basket-weave, and parquet patterns; laminated wood floors made of hardwood veneer surfaces and layers of plywood or cork; and wooden mosaic panels crafted from small blocks of wood.

Along with hardwood floors, a myriad of other hard flooring options exist, such as porous terra-cotta tiles; waterproof clay quarry tiles; ceramic tiles; mosaic tiles fashioned from glass, terra-cotta, marble, stone, or glazed clay; white, green, and blue limestone with a rough or polished surface; hard-wearing slate in blue gray, parchment, or rust; gritty, durable sandstone; elegant marble; hardwearing terrazzo, blended from a mosaic of marble chips; and slip-resistant, durable quartzite in grays, buff, greens, or black. While natural clay and stone flooring can add rich textures and patterns to your rooms, be aware that these materials can be costly, and they're not noise or heat insulators.

Floor Coverings   Coir is coconut fiber that is often woven into sturdy, easy-to-clean doormats. Jute matting is created from yarn made from the jute plant; it is soft but difficult to clean and impractical for heavily trafficked areas. Rush matting is made of woven rush leaves; it is elegant and expensive, and is best as an accent in spaces with little wear. Seagrass, made from a grass grown in paddy fields, is practical, easy to clean, and durable. Sisal comes from the subtropical agave sisalana bush; its yarn can be dyed to make solid or multicolored floor coverings that are durable and come in a variety of textures. Wool-based natural floor coverings are created from woven wool and nylon or sisal; they are a cross between natural floor coverings and carpet, and their advantage lies in their soft textures and easily cleaned surfaces. Wool carpeting is durable and luxurious, and has a wonderful depth of color, but it is harder to keep clean than most synthetic carpets.

Paneling   Wood paneling can add warmth to any room of the home, from bedroom to bath, living room to home office. The most common woods for paneling are economical softwoods such as pine, while more expensive hardwoods, including maple, cedar, walnut, and redwood, are sometimes chosen for their rich patina, which improves with age. Softwood paneling is often beautified with varnish, wood stain, or paint. Whatever wood paneling you choose, you'll benefit from its timeless looks, and heat and sound insulation.

Natural Paints   Nowadays a wide spectrum of synthetic, water-based latex paint and oil-based paint is available in finishes from matte to high gloss. Still, some homeowners around the world are rediscovering paints featuring natural pigments derived from earth, clay, or rock. Organic paint lends the luminous colors of nature to interior walls and facades in such old-world places as Provence and Tuscany. Iron oxide creates ocher in a range of yellows, browns, reds, and oranges. Iron silicate produces terre verte, a moss green pigment. Violets and blues are derived from manganese dioxide, while reds and oranges come from cadmium. The advantage of natural pigments is that they create lush, softly patchy antique matte finishes that subtly change as a room's natural light changes. The challenge is that they require skillful mixing to avoid a splotchy result. They also require special handling, as these pigments stain and must not be inhaled or ingested.

Furnishings and Fabrics   Because the planet's rain forests are endangered, it's good to buy furniture made of wood from local, sustainable forests that are continually replanted. Softwoods such as pine, fir, and larch, and hardwoods such as beech, poplar, maple, oak, ash, and walnut are good choices, since there is a conscientious effort to maintain these species through replanting. Woods that are harder to replenish include teak and mahogany. Other popular natural materials used for home furnishings are bamboo, rattan, and cane, to name a few. Even stone can be used indoors, though it is best suited for substantial pieces such as tables.

Floors fashioned from wood, clay, limestone, slate, or brick add color and natural texture to the home. The timeless stone floor of this guest bedroom contrasts beautifully with the smooth woods, rough woven fabrics, and sleek contemporary lighting and window treatments.

Natural fabrics offer an exciting range of textures, colors, and patterns that add beauty to the peaceful home. Popular choices with a wide variety of uses include long-lasting linen (which is available in a range of weaves, coarse through fine); versatile, colorful cottons in a variety of weights, such as gauzy muslin, ticking, madras, and duck; shiny luxurious silks in textures ranging from smooth chiffon to uneven shantung; and hessian (more commonly known as burlap), a rough fabric made from jute or a mixture of hemp and jute. The sheer variety of natural fabrics available ensures that there is something just right for every decor.

OPPOSITE: By filling your rooms with things that reflect your passions and joys, such as fresh-cut flowers, heirloom furnishings, and favorite artwork, you personalize your environment, making it a warm and welcoming place for family as well as friends.

ABOVE: From breathable cottons to nubby chenille, a wide variety of contemporary and vintage textiles are available to lend beauty, comfort, and pleasing texture to restful retreats. This bedroom's neutral palette is enlivened by the woven headboard, the tropical motif curtains, and the playful zebra print above the chaise.

PEACEFUL PLEASURES

Wallpaper Creates Rooms with a View

English Arts and Crafts visionary William Morris once said, "Whatever you have in your rooms, think first of the walls . . . which make your house a home." A decorative element in ancient Chinese and medieval European dwellings, wallpaper's magic can whisk us away to other times and places, as well as transform our favorite rooms with touchable textures, intriguing patterns, and soothing colors. Here are a few nature-inspired wall covering ideas:

- Embossed wallpapers add warmth and camouflage flaws in your walls. Designs include simulated wood grain and floral designs.
- Faux wallpapers decorate your rooms with fool-the-eye marble, tiles, fine wood, leather, rock, and semi-precious stones.
- Wallpapers of natural material such as woven grass cloth (made of grass and reeds affixed to a paper backing) are available in a variety of colors. Wall coverings made from jute and hemp also create evocative neutral-colored backdrops.

- Wallpapers that simulate fabric resemble such materials as raw silk, flecked linen, and burlap.
- Machine-printed wallpapers with nature-inspired designs include flora and fauna motifs, celestial panoramas, seashore vignettes, scenic woodlands, and desert and mountain landscapes.
- Borders and friezes are available in a variety of styles and textures. They are traditionally used to accent walls by acting as molding at the ceiling or wainscoting at midwall.

OPPOSITE: In this bathroom, the gentle hues of the walls and the lovely stone tiles on the floor and shower stall provide a neutral canvas for a shower curtain created from vibrant Japanese fabrics. The natural materials and colors in the room create a connection to the forest visible through the large windows.

ABOVE: Stylized floral-patterned papers, such as this one by Bradbury and Bradbury, are perfect for an Arts and Crafts decor.

SERENE DECORS: AN ARTS AND CRAFTS ENTRY HALL AND LIVING ROOM

The unpretentious designs of Arts and Crafts furnishings call attention to the rich colors, textures, and patterns of nature. In an authentically detailed Arts and Crafts–style home, the nature-inspired front hallway immediately embraces visitors and family. The floor may be flagstone or wood, topped by an Oriental runner, while the walls feature a lush wallpaper pattern designed by William Morris. A small oak trestle table protected by a hand-embroidered table runner serves as a catchall for keys and mail. Atop the table is an art pottery vase filled with native flowers and a hammered-copper lamp with a translucent mica shade. The table is flanked by two Mission oak chairs with cushions in muted, earthy hues. On one wall is a hand-carved wooden hat rack, while a large beveled mirror framed in oak graces the wall over the trestle table.

Down the hall, serenity reigns in the living room where the rich oak paneling reflects the burning embers of a fire in the grand stone or tile fireplace. The ceiling is painted white and highlighted with oak beams. A lush floral or geometric-patterned carpet adds color to the dark plank floor. Facing the fireplace is a large Mission-style armchair or rocker topped by earth-toned pillows. Other furnishings include several small oak and chestnut wooden tables, a few straight, square Stickley chairs with visible pegs and wood joints, and a walnut secretary with leaded-glass windows revealing a collection of art pottery and antique books. Texturally inviting accessories include several stained-glass lamps, a few heavily framed landscape paintings, and several wrought-iron candle holders.

A fireplace of hand-painted tiles in earthy hues is the focal point of this cozy living room, which perfectly re-creates the style of the Arts and Crafts movement. A Mission-style rocker and matching armchair of solid oak are pulled close to the fire to enjoy the warmth of the blaze. The beautiful wood is also used to panel the walls, frame the windows, and form the built-in bench and leaded-glass-fronted cabinets.

75

Old-world romance is suggested in this lavishly appointed living room, where walls seem to shimmer like gold as natural light filters through the room. Although somewhat challenging to work with, natural paint pigments are revered for their antique matte finishes, which delight both the eye and the soul.

PEACEFUL PLEASURES

Simple Ways to Bring Nature Indoors

Poet William Wordsworth bared his soul when he wrote, "Nature never did betray the heart that loved her." Express your passion for the countryside by inviting nature into your home with these easy, enriching decorating touches:

- Consider leaving lovely windows undressed if privacy isn't a concern. Sometimes unadorned windows are the most elegant of all.
- String tiny seashells or preserved autumn leaves together and drape these garlands over simple mirrors or doorways.
- Find room for a small indoor fountain that can add tranquility with its soothing sounds and gentle, moving water.
- Create a garden indoors with a series of framed botanical prints
- Spotlight a landscape painting or a series of framed nature photos by placing them close to the room's focal point: above a fireplace or atop a piano or carved antique table.
- Display fresh flowers picked from your garden or bought at the market, a nearby florist, or a good supermarket.
- Nurture an indoor garden of plants of various sizes, shapes, and colors; they'll look lovely in terra-cotta or decorative china planters.
- Force bulbs such as paperwhites or autumn crocus in glass or hand-made pottery vessels to fill your rooms with natural beauty and fragrance during the winter months.

RELAXING WITH SOOTHING FURNISHINGS AND ACCESSORIES

"I'd love to see less and less studied decoration and more things chosen because you love them. That's the whole point, really."

—Billy Baldwin

In one respect, you and I are like the bold little girl in "Goldilocks and the Three Bears." We care deeply about physical comfort—we know what feels just right—and we search hungrily until we find it. Just as a hug from a loved one or a nuzzle from our dog or cat can warm us after a hard day, we can also feel soothed by the soft embrace of a sofa or an antique rocker that we've known for ages. We become attached to our favoritechairs, sofas, tables, and, of course, our beds, which provide sanctuary for sweet dreams, heartfelt conversations, and reveling in good books.

A graceful chair upholstered in golden velveteen provides a soft, pleasing contrast to the strong lines of the wrought-iron table in this cozy corner. A curvaceous brass candelabra and a jointed wooden artist's model of a hand add personality to the space.

The rounded edges and plush upholstery of these sectional couches soften the crisp, clean lines of the architecture in this living room, making it a warm and inviting place to visit with friends in front of a roaring fire.

Linda Marder, principle designer of Linda Marder, a Los Angeles–based interior design firm, says, "We only have so many opportunities to be comfortable. I say let's take them all. That's why I design rooms with a lot of upholstered pieces. As far as accessories go, I love one hundred percent down pillows; they're soft and squishy and seem to

disappear when you sit down." Ms. Marder suggests that soothing materials and textures also have a rightful place in our most private oases. "We spend so much time in our bedrooms," she notes, "so we should make the bed as cozy as possible. If my clients will let me, I design sumptuous beds for them with big down comforters, soft chenille

Renowned architect Frank Lloyd Wright said, "If you wisely invest in beauty, it will remain with you all the days of your life." This living room's elegant upholstered furnishings, subtly textured apricot walls, and fine antiques all speak of luxury and exquisite craftsmanship, two components of a blissful, cherished room.

throws, and vintage cotton bed sheets, the older the better. And in the bathroom, touches like electric towel warmers can evoke the feeling of being at a fabulous luxury hotel."

According to architect and author Witold Rybczynski, furniture has always had both utilitarian and symbolic functions. Ages ago, however, physical comfort wasn't always uppermost in craftsmen's minds. From the thirteenth through the fifteenth centuries, when monasteries dominated the medieval world's advances in the arts, medicine, science, and technology, ecclesiastical-inspired Gothic furniture imitated the religious architecture of the times. Severe, straight-backed pews and hard benches were designed for commoners, while towering straight-backed chairs with hard seats were reserved for those in authority. To the monks, uncomfortable furnishings were a way for people to be wakeful in church and mindful of self-sacrifice.

Fortunately, times have changed. Furniture is now designed for comfort, convenience, and beauty. If you take a

moment to admire the craftsmanship of a favorite chair in your home, you can appreciate its classic lines or flair, and be reminded of all the times you sat in it cuddling your child, visiting with friends, or getting lost in great novels. Perhaps the chair was a tag sale find, a family heirloom, or a gift from your beloved. To you, it's more than a chair; it's a comforting haven. In the same vein, your cherished brass bed isn't merely an antique; it's a symbol of nightly renewal and refreshment. Your bathtub speaks to you of purification, not only for your body, but for your spirit as well. By seeing your furniture and fixtures in new ways, you appreciate them for their myriad contributions to the peaceful essence of your home and your life.

Art truly imitates life in this lovely dining area. The curvaceous wooden chairs seem to mirror the limbs of the trees just outside the window, while the creatively draped window dressing adds warm color and a sense of rhythm to the enchanting setting.

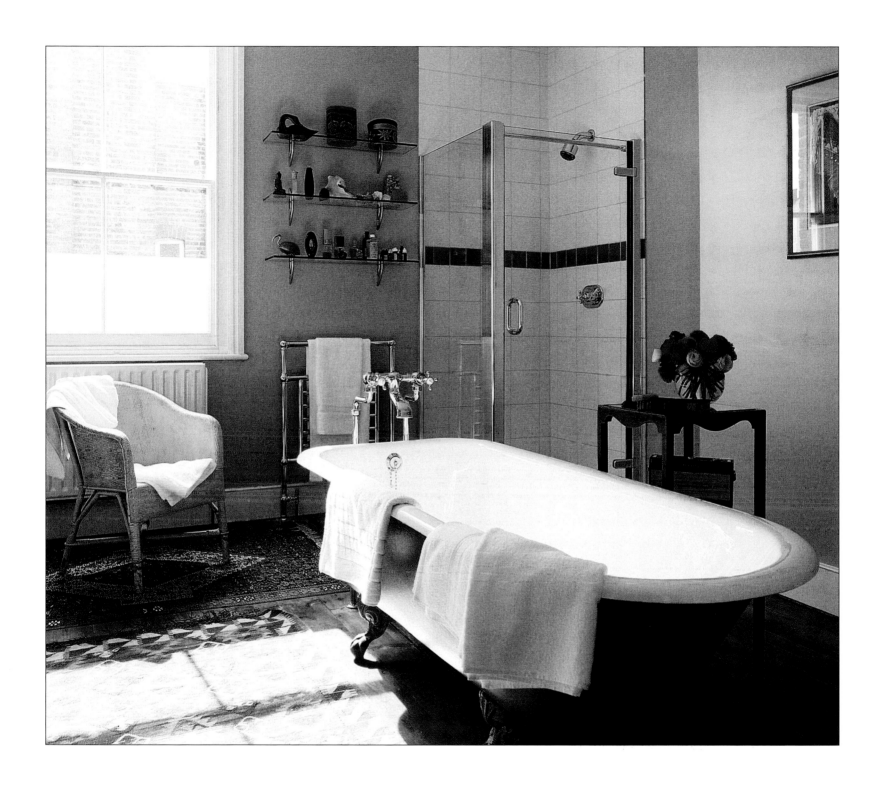

An old-fashioned claw-foot tub is the focal point of this eclectic bathroom. Walls in a cool, watery hue, plush towels, fresh flowers, and plenty of sunshine all work together to create a retreat for body, mind, and spirit.

SELECTING FURNITURE

While certain furnishings—such as upholstered chairs, sofas, and beds—are fashioned for rest and relaxation, others are designed for dining, work, or storage. In order to contribute to the peaceful aura of your rooms, furnishings and accessories must provide you not only with physical comfort and convenience, but with emotional solace as well. Would you and your family feel tranquil in a room filled with antiques or reproduction period furniture? Or would the general consensus be for a more casual, sturdy country ambience, or the clean look of contemporary furnishings? Along with considering comfort and design, it's good to decide whether the furniture will be used strictly for your family or for entertaining company, and if it needs to serve several purposes—as with a generous kitchen table that moonlights as a desk or a sofa that doubles as a bed when guests are in town.

When selecting furnishings, keep in mind construction, style, size, function, quality, and cost. Traditional furnishings are generally made of wood (oak, cherry, mahogany, pecan), metal (polished steel, cast iron), natural fibers (bamboo, willow, wicker), and such other earthly resources

A sense of order and well-being prevails in uncluttered rooms filled with favorite furnishings and accessories. This minimalist living room with Oriental flair honors the ancient Chinese practice of feng shui by utilizing natural light, carefully placed mirrors, and the harmonious elements of wood (seen in the table, chairs, and floor) and fire (embodied by the orange pillows).

84

FURNISHINGS AND ACCESSORIES

SELECTING FURNITURE

While certain furnishings—such as upholstered chairs, sofas, and beds—are fashioned for rest and relaxation, others are designed for dining, work, or storage. In order to contribute to the peaceful aura of your rooms, furnishings and accessories must provide you not only with physical comfort and convenience, but with emotional solace as well. Would you and your family feel tranquil in a room filled with antiques or reproduction period furniture? Or would the general consensus be for a more casual, sturdy country ambience, or the clean look of contemporary furnishings? Along with considering comfort and design, it's good to decide whether the furniture will be used strictly for your family or for entertaining company, and if it needs to serve several purposes—as with a generous kitchen table that moonlights as a desk or a sofa that doubles as a bed when guests are in town.

When selecting furnishings, keep in mind construction, style, size, function, quality, and cost. Traditional furnishings are generally made of wood (oak, cherry, mahogany, pecan), metal (polished steel, cast iron), natural fibers (bamboo, willow, wicker), and such other earthly resources

A sense of order and well-being prevails in uncluttered rooms filled with favorite furnishings and accessories. This minimalist living room with Oriental flair honors the ancient Chinese practice of feng shui by utilizing natural light, carefully placed mirrors, and the harmonious elements of wood (seen in the table, chairs, and floor) and fire (embodied by the orange pillows).

PEACEFUL PLEASURES

The Bliss of the Bedroom

If you're like most adults, you spend anywhere from a quarter to a third of each day sleeping. That's why your bed should embrace you with comfort and luxury. Your bedroom itself should feel like a dreamy, soothing sanctuary for slumber, meditation, and romance. Keep these thoughts in mind when decorating your bedroom:

- When buying your bed, remember that it's your room's focal point. Favorite romantic styles include four-poster beds with canopies or drapes, ornamental iron beds that can be accented with silky coronets suspended above, and curvaceous wooden sleigh beds.

- Experts advise buying your mattress and box spring together to ensure the most comfortable system available. When selecting your mattress, lie down in a sleeping position to truly know if it suits your needs. If you share your bed, be sure to have your partner test the bed at the same time.

- A captivating headboard can be made from such unique items as a leaded- or stained-glass window, a piece of salvaged architectural ornamentation, a vintage fireplace mantel, a decorative folding screen, or a hanging quilt.

- Dress your bed with pure linen or quality all-cotton sheets. The higher the thread count (number of threads woven into each square inch of cloth), the more luxurious the fabric.

- In a pinch, you may be tempted to park stacks of books, boxes, or sports equipment in your bedroom corner.

- Resist the urge. Clutter creates an air of chaos, not serenity. Instead, count on closet shelving and underbed bins for extra storage space.

- If you have children, consider installing a bedroom door lock for privacy.

- Dimmer-controlled lighting isn't just for the dining room—it can add enticing ambience to your bedroom. Another cozy idea is pink light bulbs. And, of course, a variety of scented candles can bring a magical glow to the night.

- Tuck away TV and stereo equipment in an armoire or cabinet. And remember that soft music can soothe and caress you.

- Consider hanging wind chimes near your window or placing a small indoor fountain and plants on a bedside table. Either will add gentle, tranquil sound and beauty.

- Introduce the fragrances of nature through fresh flowers, bowls of potpourri, scented candles, eucalyptus swags, or bunches of dried herbs or flowers from your garden.

As author Mark Twain discovered more than a century ago, a beautifully designed bed can become a hideaway where the solace of favorite colors, cozy bedding, fresh breezes, and sweet dreams melt away all your cares.

as marble, porcelain, leather, glass, and alabaster. As furnishings are a major expenditure, you'll want to buy pieces that are made to last. You should also select pieces that suit your taste, needs, and budget and that will fit into your decor, both physically and aesthetically. Serene environments radiate a sense of spaciousness, so when you shop you'll want to bring along your room measurements and a measuring tape to make sure there's ample space in your home for the pieces that you fall in love with.

Just as you do your homework and visit several dealerships before investing in a new car, it's wise to read home decorating magazines and to visit furniture showrooms to window shop and ask the sales staff about furniture construction, upholstery, and pricing before you purchase anything. You'll likely see a wide variety of reproductions (detailed copies of fine antiques), collections (related furniture pieces that can be purchased separately or as a group), adaptations (inspired by certain furnishing styles),

Searching at antique shows and flea markets can uncover lovely furnishings, paintings, and accessories that can make decorating your home an exciting adventure. Here, choice pieces from the Arts and Crafts period, namely the simple, handcrafted sideboard and the graceful pottery vessels, help create a soothing and harmonious room.

This masterfully carved table is a testament to the gracious personality and history of antique furnishings. Perched atop the table are three bowls containing stylized carved fish. Each watery sphere lends color and surprise.

sectional furniture (pieces that come in sections that are designed to fit together, such as a sectional sofa), smaller apartment-sized pieces, and possibly some ready-to-assemble (RTA) furniture.

The assortment of decorating fabrics that you'll discover throughout home-furnishing stores is exciting. Chenille—which means caterpillar in French—yields fuzzy cotton bedspreads and decadent, lush throws and pillows for sofas and beds. Flannel, a soft, smooth material made from wool or cotton, is used for upholstery and bed linens, as well as everyone's favorite cozy shirts. Transparent cotton gauze is popular for sheer bed draperies and window treatments. Linen is a long-lasting natural fabric that gets softer with use, which is why it is favored for summery slipcovers, elegant sheets, guest towels, and tablecloths. Ottoman is a lustrous, horizontally ribbed upholstery fabric that's often made of silk and cotton. Silk is elegant but not necessarily extravagant;

pure silk and silk blends are used to create shimmering bedspreads, draperies, cushions, and upholstery. Soft as a pansy petal, velvet's thick, dense pile can be created from silk, cotton, or rayon; it's used for pillows, draperies, slipcovers, and upholstery. Wool is ideal for upholstery, draperies, blankets, and throws. Wool products come from a variety of sheep and lambs, Angora goats (which produce mohair) and Angora rabbits, Kashmir goats, alpacas, and camels.

The comfort level you feel with your furniture will be influenced not only by the pieces themselves but by their placement in your home. Keep in mind that intimate groupings or "islands" of furniture can create serene spaces. Furniture can also be arranged symmetrically, asymmetrically, or radially, and a large piece such as an armoire, a tall bookcase, or a kitchen dresser needn't hug your walls when it might look more dynamic standing diagonally in a corner.

Each of the six decorating styles highlighted throughout this book offers its own superior examples of elegantly comfortable furniture. For example, in an Arts and Crafts decor, sumptuous leather chairs and upholstered sofas covered in William Morris–style flora and fauna prints provide sublime luxury. On the other hand, in the eclectic setting, a variety of traditional- or country-style furniture such as neoclassical Grecian recliners or polished wooden rocking chairs promise comfort, while in a Japanese decor, a soft futon for sleeping or a silk-cushioned bamboo chair can become the lap of luxury.

Rooted in tradition, this eclectic bedroom successfully mixes an antique four-poster bed, a vintage lamp, and a gossamer window treatment with a one-of-a-kind contemporary painting.

Scouting for Accessories

Part of the fun of decorating your home is the thrill of the hunt. It takes time to find just the right accessories, and you can relish the weekend and vacation outings that lead you to little nuggets that add life and memories to your rooms. Just as fashion accessories such as shoes and jewelry add drama to your wardrobe, carefully chosen accessories can accentuate the walls, corners, furnishings, and focal points of your decor. Paintings, wall hangings, prints, pillows, luxurious throws, candle holders, plants, framed photos, vases, mirrors, and wreaths are all popular accessories. Art galleries and shows are good places to find these items, as are museum gift shops, crafts and collectible shows, flea markets, antiques shops, and department stores. Beaches are great spots to find beautiful seashells and driftwood and washed-up shards of pottery and colored glass, while camping trips will provide you with pinecones of all sizes for holiday displays.

Serene Decors: Cottage-style Bedrooms

Furniture not only radiates personality in our rooms, it's been called the foundation of our decors. In the cottage-style home, an assortment of vintage, new, and garden furnishings can collaborate to create a symphony of charm and tranquility. In the master bedroom, key furnishings might include a stripped-pine four-poster bed topped with a muted rose, buttercup, sage, and ivory antique quilt and a sheer muslin canopy, and two plump easy chairs covered with linen slipcovers and a few pillows

The star of this sun-kissed sanctuary is the hand-forged iron bed, a focal point that speaks of a reverence for soaring Gothic cathedrals and castles. An island of comfort, the pristine bed is surrounded by a sea of pale wooden flooring, white stucco walls, and fragrant flowers— all adding to the room's ambience of romance and tranquility.

In the cottage bedroom, a variety of simple furnishings crafted from wood, wicker, brass, or iron are fitting. Here, a tropical cane bed blends artfully with softly patterned bed linens, fresh fruits and flowers, a beautiful sepia print, and timeless stucco walls.

space, and, by the room's lace-curtained window, an ornamental green garden glider topped with creamy linen cushions. The wainscoted walls and the ceiling would feature ivory-hued beadboard, while the wallpaper from wainscoting to ceiling level would evoke Victoriana with its muted yellow, raspberry, and sage cabbage rose wallpaper. The wooden floor would be topped with neutral sisal matting.

A child's restful cottage-style bedroom could feature neutral- or cool-colored beadboard wainscoting with a coordinating wall color painted above, perhaps cheery yellow or calm blue, green, or lavender. As the child grows, this color scheme could be changed simply with a fresh coat of paint and new accessories such as pillows, bedspreads, and curtains. Children's walls can also be decorated with colorful stick-on wallpaper borders that can be peeled off easily when redecorating. The focal point of this youthful cottagey bedroom would be a brass or iron twin-sized bed topped with a teddy bear–soft chenille bedspread or down-filled comforter. Other furnishings would include a solid stripped-pine or maple dresser (both woods are durable and aren't marred by everyday nicks and scratches); a stripped-pine or maple desk, chair, and bookshelf; a wicker toy trunk (the lid is lighter than a wooden one and easier for little fingers to lift); a comforting slipcovered loveseat for sharing bedtime stories; and a brightly colored rag rug on the pine plank floor.

fashioned from faded chintz, gingham, and vintage floral handkerchiefs. The chairs would be positioned around the room's small fireplace. Its cream-colored wooden mantel would display a few family photos and a rustic basket of fresh flowers. Other furnishings would include a cream-colored beadboard cabinet that hides a stereo system, an 1890s pastel green "cottage furniture" dresser with pink cabbage roses painted on its drawers, a vintage gilded mirror, a stripped-pine armoire for extra storage

The Victorian penchant for summers spent by the sea is suggested in this refreshingly cool-hued cottage bathroom. The walls have been painted a robin's egg blue to contrast with the crisp white of the tiles and trim. The decorative lacy valance reminiscent of a parasol and the carved molding above the bathtub provide texture, pattern, and a sense of days gone by.

PEACEFUL PLEASURES

Sensuous Bathrooms

While your powder room pampers your visitors, the master or family bathroom can be your private getaway for luxurious steamy showers or long soaks in the tub. Here are a few ideas for enhancing the serenity of the room where you greet the dawn and unwind at day's end:

- Redo your walls with colors that calm and soothe you, such as soft robin's-egg blue, emerald green, seafoam, lavender, or silver. Choose from a wide variety of high-gloss mildew-resistant paint, water-repellent vinyl wallpaper, painted or stained beadboard paneling, or elegant marble or ceramic tiles.

- Cover your floors with waterproof vinyl tiles or slip-resistant ceramic tiles, topped with plush bathroom rugs that have a nonskid backing. The rugs will massage your feet with warmth and texture on chilly mornings.

- Typical bathroom lighting includes a ceiling fixture and lights on either side of the vanity mirror. Other options include recessed incandescent fixtures with dimmer controls for creating a darker, more relaxed ambience, and a skylight—a perfect way to introduce healing sunshine to a windowless room.

- Decorative sinks can add an elegant country, period, or contemporary flair to your decor. Delightful to see and touch, today's sinks are created from porcelain, stainless steel, stone, bronze, glass, cast iron, and even wood. Alluring styles include recessed sinks in vanity cabinets, pedestal sinks, and raised "washbasin style" vessels in a wide variety of shapes, designs, and opulent colors.

- Reproduction claw-foot bathtubs are so beautiful, they're often considered sculpture for the bathroom. Such tubs are made from stainless steel, enameled cast iron, and copper. They're especially inviting when placed by a window with a view.

- Contemporary cast-iron, fiberglass, or glossy acrylic tubs come in a plethora of colors and shapes. Fitting bathing accessories include vinyl bath pillows, velvety towels, fragrant bath oils, and, for romantics, several scented candles for a relaxing glow.

- State-of-the-art hydro-massage systems can create a revitalizing custom home shower. These systems provide numerous water jets that can be adjusted to massage the body with gentle or intense water flow to ease tired muscles and rejuvenate both body and spirit.

CHAPTER FIVE

PERSONALIZING YOUR ROOMS WITH SACRED TREASURES

"We do not remember days, we remember moments."

—Cesare Pavese

You may not think of special accessories as treasures, but they are. Photographs are the next best thing to time travel, for they enable you to gaze again at a loved one's precious smile or twinkling eyes, or to be transported to your favorite mountain or seaside haven. Tabletop vignettes of several framed family photos are a wonderful way to add an intimate sense of heart and soul to your home. Countless other articles—from a smooth conch shell to the pastel sketch that you drew once upon a time of your sleeping baby—can rekindle tender memories, and add a youthful glow to your rooms.

Sweet dreams are assured in this tranquil blue and white bedroom where sunlight and moonlight dance across a cozy bed protected by a dream catcher. According to the ancient Ojibwe (Chippewa) nation, originators of the dream catcher, this colorful Native American artifact encourages good dreams to slip through its center hole, while bad dreams become entangled in the webbing, disappearing with the dawn.

Interior designer Stephanie Cattarin suggests, "You should surround yourself with items that you love, such as a favorite wedding present, a flea market collectible you just had to have, or an heirloom handed down from your great-grandmother. If these objects evoke a warm memory or remind you of a funny story, you're going to feel happy, and in turn, you'll feel at peace with your home and yourself." Ellen White Weir, owner of Homescapes, a home-furnishing store and interior design service in Cooperstown, New York, shares a similar outlook. "People have collections because they want connections to the past," she says, "and a sense of the familiar breeds peace."

Countless designers agree that when it comes to accessorizing your rooms, editing is critical. A few carefully chosen accessories can add beauty and tranquil personality to your rooms without making them feel cluttered or overdone. Introduce a handful of your treasures at a time, and rotate these several times a year with other favorite objects. If you're passionate about your hobby, your mementos or tools from such pastimes can be

used to make creative displays. Remember, too, that paintings, prints, photos, and wall hangings should all be placed with care. Generally, if they're displayed in a leisurely spot such as the sunroom or dining room, they should be hung just above the eye level of an adult sitting in the room. Since hallways are places for traffic flow, paintings should be positioned a bit higher, to be admired from a standing position.

OPPOSITE: When it comes to arranging similar objects, there's strength in numbers, as can be seen In this lovely array of shimmering glass apples and pears on the marble fireplace mantel.

ABOVE: This sunlit sanctuary with a window seat and luxurious bath is decorated with a personal touch. The four abstract prints on the wall lend an air of whimsical individuality to the setting.

99

A masterful landscape of enduring mountains contrasts with the ethereal beauty of fresh-picked hydrangea blossoms. The antique garden urn also adds a sense of timelessness to the mantel vignette, echoing an abiding passion for the outdoors.

When adding accessories to your rooms, remember to mix cool and warm colors to make the atmosphere inviting, and be sure to juxtapose textures and balance shapes and sizes for a sense of proportion. You'll discover that collections of small objects such as figurines, antique toys, or vintage glass bottles have more visual weight and impact when grouped together rather than scattered throughout a room. When displaying items of varying sizes, such as a group of white candles, you

can create visual verve by placing tall tapers next to wider conical, square, and pyramid-shaped candles of different heights. Fortunately, color can always be counted on to link your accessories. A living room's fireplace mantel display of blue and white porcelain can be echoed in the room's blue and gold Oriental rug and the blue paisley pillows on the sofa.

When spring turns to summer, or autumn's harvest signals the coming of winter, it's invigorating to renew your rooms with a variety of seasonal or holiday accessories. In the spring, you may want to bring out your needlepoint pillows with flower or animal designs, while in summer you reintroduce white slipcovers and a floral appliqué quilt. In the autumn, you might scatter earth-toned pillows, brass and copper lanterns, and warm Navajo throws throughout your rooms, while in December you could hang swags of evergreen boughs and holly and fill your home with tapers, in honor of Hanukkah or Christmas.

PEACEFUL PLEASURES

The Intriguing History of the Altar

From Judaism to Christianity, Buddhism to Islam, Taoism to Baha'i, our world is home to numerous religions. Despite diverse teachings, all are guiding lights that offer healing rituals and ceremonies—and the altar is just one common element that many of them share.

The word *altar* is derived from the Latin word *altus*, meaning "high." In primitive times, people would place offerings on the ground for spirits of the dead and deities of the underworld. Later, when trees, springs, or rocks were thought to be inhabited by a spirit or were considered sacred places where a god might be contacted, higher altars on which to place gifts to these deities came into being. In the Old Testament, early Hebrew altars are described as being made of earth or hewn stone for sacrifice of burnt offerings. By the first millennium, altars with projections at each corner were common. Their projections, or "horns," were often coated with sacrificial blood, and people seeking sanctuary grasped them for their sacred powers.

While some Westerners may consider the creation of home altars to be a modern ritual, it's actually an ancient tradition. For thousands of years, Hindus have presented daily offerings of flowers, incense, rice, milk, and water at their household shrines or altars, which are adorned with statues of gods and goddesses. Long ago, Greeks and Romans also placed altars in their homes, as well as in temples, public buildings, marketplaces, streets, and sacred groves in the countryside. Early altars were fashioned from elevated earth, mounds of ashes, or stacks of stones, but from the sixth century B.C. on, many of these altars were created from highly ornamented marble. The royal altars of kings and queens were often built of prized woods such as ebony or cedar, and were lavishly decorated with precious jewels, silver and gold, and luxurious fabrics. Greek and Roman altars were frequently round, while Jewish and Oriental altars were oblong or square. In early Christian churches from about 250 A.D. on, the altars were simple wooden communion tables.

CREATING A TRANQUIL ALTAR

Interior designer Linda Marder has designed altars for numerous clients, including the Los Angeles eatery–music hall House of Blues. She finds altars so comforting that she has created one in her own home. Displayed on a bedroom nightstand, it includes five statues of Buddha, an elephant-headed Ganesh (the Indian god of protection), and a lavish Russian icon of Mary and Jesus Christ. Like Ms. Marder, more and more people are awakening to the soothing beauty and spiritual significance of home altars.

While some altars inspire religious prayer and contemplation, others are collections of meaningful personal objects, such as photos of loved ones, mementos from childhood, a prayer journal, a picture or statue of an animal totem (a symbol of a revered animal guardian such as an eagle, wolf, or lion), treasured rocks and seashells, or pieces of jewelry that together paint a profound tableau that inspires meditation or promotes thoughts of gratitude, serenity, or sacred worship. Today, altars can be found everywhere, from bedrooms to kitchens, hallways to home offices, private gardens to porches. They are popular with people of traditional faiths such as Christianity or Buddhism, as well as followers of various New Age beliefs.

This Gothic cathedral–inspired living room is an idyllic spot for reflection. The room's serene sky blue walls, warm, golden light, and old-world religious icons suggest a centuries-old tradition of meditation and prayer.

Like miniature stepping-stones, this cherished collection of pebbles from the sea is appropriately displayed on a marble table. Vintage paintings, a gilded lamp, and the pebbles add warmth to this private sanctuary.

Creating an altar is an enlightening activity that symbolizes the longings of your spirit. While there are no set rules for fashioning your altar, there are common threads that are woven into the experience. The first is selecting an appropriate place in your home—a public or private room, or perhaps a sunlit or shadowed corner. Your placement might be in step with feng shui directives to enhance the chi, or energy, of your altar, or in tune with the cardinal points (north, south, east, and west) of the native American medicine wheel. The medicine wheel is a spiritual way of seeing the interconnections and energy of all earthly beings and places. You can use these traditions for inspiration or simply be guided by your own personal desires. Ideal spots for an altar can include a dresser top, bookshelf, mantel, hearth, library table, trunk, or plant stand.

Since a home altar represents the spiritual self, the items that adorn it should reflect your soul, bring you peace, and remind you of the sources of beauty, love, and energy that empower you. What will you set upon your altar? Meaningful items that lend serenity and radiance can include statuary of divine deities from specific religious traditions or of

The softly spotlighted pottery, sculptures, and other international artifacts in this curio cabinet add color, texture, pattern, and a grand sense of adventure to the room. Such personal mementos can reflect unforgettable moments of a life's journey.

patron saints or angels (often used as an altar focal point); carved replicas of animal totems; natural jewels such as sand dollars, seashells, rocks, semiprecious stones, or crystals; glowing candles and fragrant incense; photographs; jewelry and beads; vases of garden blooms; small stained-glass ornaments or windows; and decorative cloths in hues that remind you of the earth, ocean, sky, spirituality, love, or purity. Fabric stores have a vast array of silks, velvets, and velours that can add rich texture and color to your altar. For a more exotic ambience, there are luxurious woven tablecloths and bedspreads imported from India and other Asian countries. These include reproduction hand-loomed cloth with shining golden strands. Some people prefer to cover their altars with Japanese *obi* (stunning embroidered or brocaded silk or synthetic ceremonial sashes worn with

kimonos) or *furoshiki* (multipurpose decorative cotton, silk, or synthetic Japanese wrapping cloths). Even textiles from the linen closet—such as vintage lace tablecloths, doilies, or elegant woven or embroidered table runners—can make lovely altar cloths.

Building an altar takes reflection and time, but once it's completed, its peaceful presence will remind you of the blessings of your life. As poet and cultural anthropologist Joseph Campbell said, "Your sacred space is where you find yourself again and again."

This contemporary dining room with a Japanese spirit evokes thoughts of the new life and rebirth that occur each spring. The artfully displayed plants emerging from egg-shaped pottery, as well as the woven chairs, textured walls, and bamboo blinds, help blur the line between the home's inner and outer landscapes.

PEACEFUL PLEASURES

Refresh Your Spirit with Meditation

One of the most insightful bumper stickers of the last few decades states, "Life is fragile, handle with prayer."
That's good advice for both body and soul.

Recent medical studies on the power of faith suggest that repetitive prayer oftentimes can lower blood pressure and help slow breathing and heart rates. Meditation, like prayer, is also said to offer a myriad of physical benefits. In fact, meditation can trigger your body to release chemicals that help fight the "stress chemicals" that are created by angry, hostile feelings.

Simply defined, meditation is a reflective process that is designed to lead individuals to higher levels of consciousness and, sometimes, to profound states of relaxation. Today, it is a popular stress-management technique that can be used to help the body heal and repair itself. In fact, meditation reportedly may help lessen a variety of health problems, including back pain, anxiety, sleep disorders, and depression. To many people, meditation also can be used as a powerful tool for personal or spiritual development. In the home or garden, all that's needed to sit and enjoy a peaceful meditative experience is a calm, quiet environment with a comfortable rug, cushion, chair, or bed.

Interestingly, along with still or "static" meditation, there are meditation techniques based on intricate movements of the body. These include yoga, the whirling dances of Sufi dervishes, and tai chi. Each of these traditions is complex and takes time to master under the guidance of a teacher, but the benefits are well worth the effort. Many gyms, dance studios, and continuing-education centers now offer yoga and tai chi classes, so check your local paper or phone book for more information. A simpler technique that involves movement is the Zen meditation known as *kin hin*, which involves slowly walking and breathing in sync with each step. No matter what form of meditation appeals to you, there are many helpful books available to guide you in the various techniques and benefits of this peaceful pastime.

In the home office, colorful paintings and knickknacks, as well as comfortable furnishings and adequate lighting, can help create a mood of ease and efficiency. This casual home office benefits not only from overhead and task lighting, but from abundant natural light, fresh air, and an inspiring garden view.

This charming home office is really a corner of a bedroom. A revolving bookcase keeps favorite volumes close at hand, and the items on the table speak of the owner's love of travel in exotic lands.

SERENE DECORS: THE ECLECTIC HOME OFFICE

Like old friends, cherished personal accessories magically warm and lighten every room in your home, including the home office. In a cheerful home office with an eclectic personality, furnishings might include an antique Victorian oak rolltop desk that conceals a laptop, phone, fax machine, and office supplies; a hunter green wicker armchair with cozy cushions; a reproduction Victorian oak bookshelf; and a rustic plant stand fashioned from twigs and vines. This mix of formal Victorian and rustic cottage furnishings creates a relaxed summery ambience, enhanced by a yellow and green color theme, and vintage collectibles of outdoor life.

The office walls are done in a cottagey yellow beadboard paneling with a white beadboard ceiling and the room's two windows feature white wooden shutters. Overhead, the central light fixture is a white Victorian globe attached to a wooden paddle fan. Several brass lamps with simple cream-colored pleated shades offer incandescent task lighting throughout the office. A green, scarlet, and gold Oriental rug warms the woodplank floor, while green and yellow floral cushions add back support to the wicker desk chair.

Key accessories displayed on the bookshelves include reference books, a few hand-carved fish and duck decoys, and several poignant family photos set in rustic twig frames. Perhaps one office wall features a birchbark-framed nineteenth-century print of a woman and man in a canoe, while another wall displays two antique canoe paddles. Several lush green plants in Oriental porcelain pots grace the plant stand by one of the windows. The nostalgic family photos and vintage furnishings and accessories all celebrate simpler times, creating a relaxing sanctuary for work and daydreams—far from the noise, hectic pace, and lackluster decor of many corporate offices.

CHAPTER SIX

ENHANCING TRANQUILITY WITH LIGHTING, SOUND, AND FRAGRANCE

"Stay, stay at home, my heart and rest;

Home-keeping hearts are happiest."

—Henry Wadsworth Longfellow

When asked for a few helpful tips about creating a room that radiates serenity, Los Angeles interior designer Barbara Barry, ASID, of Barbara Barry, Inc., suggested, "Reduce the room to its essentials. Choose many similar shades of the same color family. Always have lamplight, even in the kitchen and bathroom. Have something polished to be the jewelry of the room . . . and always, a fresh, clean scent."

Fresh flowers can bring color and a sense of vitality to any corner of the house. In this home, a vintage urn filled with white and purple flowers provides invisible yet endearing comfort and sensual pleasure.

Without a doubt, uncluttered, easy-on-the-eye interiors, warm lighting, and pleasant fragrances can all have a powerful impact on how comforting and inviting your home feels. Just think of the special dinners you serve at home. Chances are good that you bewitch your guests with candlelight, gentle music, and the irresistible fragrances of homemade breads, roasts, pasta sauce, fruity pies, mulled cider, and vintage wine. While such special occasions are delightful, the good feelings they inspire needn't fade away. You can always treat yourself and your family to soothing lighting, sounds, and fragrances that enchant your senses and make your home and your spirit feel more tranquil and alive.

LIGHTING

Light nourishes our bodies and spirits, affecting our moods, circadian rhythms, hormones, and overall health. Within our homes, sunlight streaming in from windows and skylights brightens our moods and literally warms our home, but the intensity of light varies with the hour, the season, and the weather. Fortunately, artificial lighting can work in harmony with the sun to provide us with the amount of illumination that we need to work, relax, and feel secure.

There are three basic types of artificial lighting. General or ambient lighting provides overall illumination for a room through ceiling or wall-mounted fixtures, chandeliers, or track or recessed lights. Task lighting is designed to help you focus on your activities, such as reading or cooking. It can be provided by portable lamps, pendant lights, and track or recessed lights. Accent lighting spotlights artwork, collections, and architectural

accents and can be created with wall-mounted fixtures as well as track and recessed lights. Incandescent bulbs for these fixtures will create a warm, yellow-white light, while tungsten-halogen bulbs produce a bright white glow. Fluorescent lights generally cast a blue-toned light, but the glow from "warm white" fluorescent bulbs resembles incandescents.

Dimmer controls are ideal for general lighting in dining rooms, bedrooms, and living rooms, not only to conserve energy, but to match the lighting to the mood and activities of the room. For example, your bathroom needs to be well lit for morning grooming, so a ceiling fixture and mirror lights are practical choices for even, shadow-free lighting. If the ceiling fixture has a dimmer control, you can transform this room into a softly lit nighttime haven for bathing and listening to music by candlelight.

While basking in the sunlight streaming through your family room windows on a winter day can be a sensual pleasure for you (and your sun- worshiping cat or dog), the intense light of summer may call for soft, diffusing curtains, blinds, or shutters. Whatever the season, there's nothing like watching a sunrise or sunset from an unfettered window— or dangling prisms from your windows so you can enjoy watching the light paint rainbows on your walls. If any of your windows have unattractive views, you can camouflage them with embossed, etched, frosted, colored, or stained glass that limits the amount of light allowed into the

Time seems to stand still in this sunroom filled with light, air, and beautiful old stone. The magnificent water fountain and urn create a simple, almost spiritual vignette, complemented by the stucco walls and textured stone floor.

Ultraviolet light can fade wooden floors and furnishings, as well as beloved artwork. Fortunately, window treatments such as shutters and shades can dramatically reduce UV rays, and provide an aesthetic way to control the amount of light filtering into each room.

This bathroom offers state-of-the-art fixtures and a sense of serenity and romance. Warm carved wood, a generous vanity for two, luminous golden walls, and poetic architectural design help make this room a sanctuary. The arched doorway leads to a balcony where views of breathtaking sunsets can be seen.

room while adding a decorative glow. For a room with little or no natural lighting, a skylight can be an energy-efficient and aesthetic solution. While lighting from a window will spotlight the periphery of a room, a skylight provides two to five times more illumination than a vertical window, efficiently lighting a room the same way an overhead ceiling fixture does.

Since ancient times, candles have been used in the home as well as in religious rituals, festivals, processions, and ceremonies. Candles of all shapes and sizes can add a golden glow to a romantic dinner, a cozy evening gathering of friends, or a private hour of meditation at your home altar. A wide variety of candle holders—including glass hurricane lamps, sconces, lanterns, small votives, and tall brass, iron, glass, wood, or ceramic candlestick holders—add serenity to any setting.

Sometimes the most dramatic accent light in any room is the natural sunlight spilling through windows and doorways. This bright corner with a casual outdoor spirit is perfect for reading, meditating, or just relaxing with a cup of tea.

116

PEACEFUL PLEASURES

Protect Your Family Against Noise Pollution

While noise can be pleasant, annoying, or just a background hum, we rarely give much thought to its harmful effects. Yet according to the National Institute on Deafness and Other Communication Disorders, approximately seven million Americans have developed serious hearing problems from overexposure to noise. Can such hearing damage occur at home? Sometimes. A general rule is that if you have to shout when you're within four feet of someone, the household noise is loud enough to cause hearing damage. Here are a few helpful tips to keep the noise level down in your home:

- Machinery such as leaf blowers or chain saws can cause problems. Earplugs are recommended when you're exposed to such noises at home or work.
- When wearing headphones, set the volume low enough so that you can hear not only the music but someone who's talking to you in a normal voice from three feet away.
- If you live near an airport or on a busy street, block outside noise by replacing single-pane windows with double or triple panes.
- For quiet floors, consider installing sound-absorbing, thick carpeting, or factory-made solid wood floors that are constructed with layered wood placed over plastic sheathing.
- To help block out noise from other rooms, replace hollow-core bedroom doors with solid-core doors.
- Sound-deadening kits are available for some appliances, such as refrigerators, washing machines, and dryers. The kits usually include rubber mounting plates or pads that help separate the appliance from the wall or floor, thus reducing banging sounds.
- In the living room or family room, the sounds of television and conversation can usually be absorbed by thick carpeting, acoustic tile, and heavy drapes.

OPPOSITE: This elegantly appointed hallway bids a gracious welcome to all who enter. When guests visit, the wonderful collection of candles is lit, making the home feel even more alive with warmth and color.

LEFT: This contemporary dining room delights the senses with radiant sunlight, lovely furnishings, rich woodwork and flooring, and the room's most memorable asset—a unique Japanese water garden that divides the room.

PEACEFUL PLEASURES

Breathe Easy Indoors

Our Victorian ancestors were right: throughout every season, fresh air is vital to a healthy body and spirit. Unfortunately, though, many of today's newer homes are so energy efficient that while cold weather drafts are kept out, humidity and indoor pollutants often build to harmful levels because they can't escape. Without proper mechanical and natural ventilation, humidity can become excessive enough to allow allergy-causing molds and mildews to thrive. Also, in airtight homes, unhealthy levels of indoor pollutants can cause serious respiratory problems. Common pollutants include cigarette smoke; formaldehyde from plywood, particle board, carpeting, drapes, and upholstery; paints and paint strippers with high levels of volatile organic compounds (VOC); toxic pesticides; aerosol grooming products such as hair sprays and deodorants; and cleaning agents such as bleach and ammonia.

Here are a few tips to help you and your family breathe easier, for peaceful and healthful days and nights:

- Select furniture for your home that is made of wood and sealed with water-based, low-VOC paints and sealers.
- Choose kitchen and bathroom counters made of glazed ceramic tile, stainless steel, or stone.
- Color your walls with low-VOC paints.
- Dress windows in easy-to-clean blinds or swags to minimize dust.
- Keep all toxic cleaning, lawn, and garden products away from the living areas of your home.
- If family members have allergies or respiratory conditions, you may benefit from a high-efficiency particle arrestor (HEPA) filter. These can be installed in most HVAC (heating, ventilating, and air-conditioning) systems to remove about ninety-eight percent of the tiny particles in your indoor air, such as pollen and spores.
- To freshen the air in a single room, a portable, self-contained electronic air cleaner can be used.
- Many houseplants provide excellent air purification. Several key types that cleanse the air by absorbing household pollutants into their leaves are spider plants, rubber plants, peace lilies, Boston ferns, and arrowhead vines.

Recent studies on the power of music have found that it can be used to enhance alertness, concentration, and a sense of well-being. A variety of gentle music, from Gregorian chants and classical works to the natural melodies of garden wind chimes, can help soothe the spirit.

the soothing sounds of Brahms or Mozart, modern troubadours such as Dan Fogelberg or James Taylor, angelic voices such as Enya or the chanting Benedictine monks of Santo Domingo de Silos, or even outdoor recordings of bird songs, crashing waves, thunder, rain, and wind. Whatever our musical preferences, we're following an ancient tradition of healing with sound, rhythm, and chanting that was practiced by the early Greeks, as well as countless cultures around the world.

Along with music, other sounds can create an atmosphere of calm and relaxation in your home. The Chinese believe that moving water brings good luck and a sense of peace. You can find countless tabletop

SOUND

To escape the cacophony of modern life—from blaring horns and sirens to construction jackhammers and jets slicing through the sky—many of us count on music to soothe our frazzled nerves. We fill our rooms with

121

fountains handmade from natural slate, river stone, pottery, marble, and copper to add the allure of cascading water to your rooms. There is also a wide variety of wind chimes available, including some that resemble ancient Chinese temple bells (which are said to attract prosperity and good fortune), and others that are precision-tuned to echo the sound of Gregorian chants. You can even find chiming alarm clocks that wake you gently, in contrast to a loud buzzer that can startle even the deepest sleeper.

FRAGRANCE

Philosopher Jean-Jacques Rousseau said, "Smell is the sense of the imagination." Indeed, your sense of smell is a magic carpet that can take you anywhere in your past, instantaneously rekindling images of a breezy summer spent by the sea, the delicious smell of your mom's pumpkin pie, your dad's famous spaghetti sauce, the spicy cologne your grandpa wore, or the pungent eucalyptus rub your grandma prescribed for chest colds.

It is said that most people can distinguish more than ten thousand different odors. Scent can powerfully affect our state of mind, as well as drive our hunger or thirst and induce feelings of vitality or unease. In ancient Egypt, Greece, and India, physicians used aromatic essences distilled from plants to combat pain and depression, improve sleep, and inspire passion. Today, the practice of aromatherapy uses essential plant oils to promote health and a sense of emotional peace. You can find a variety of aromatherapy candles, diffusers, and light bulb rings that release essential oils throughout the home. These fragrances are said to

ABOVE: The gentle sounds of wind chimes, water fountains, and chirping birds can all add to a home's sense of serenity.

OPPOSITE: Using fragrance to heighten the allure of our surroundings is a timeless tradition. In this corner, a scented candle provides tantalizing fragrance, while a beautiful crystal refracts light and adds a sense of spirituality.

This eclectic room successfully blends contemporary furnishings and crisp architectural styling with the regal presence of a classic grand piano. The proportions of each of the room's three distinct furniture groupings balance with the formal music corner. Neutral colors, rough and smooth textures, and an expansive window view create a cohesive, inviting space.

A medley of neutral tones and natural textures give this room its tranquil charm. Two comfortable sofas, upholstered in a flax-colored fabric, face one another across the marble-topped table. A natural fiber rug grounds the room, while the watercolor above the fireplace provides a splash of color.

brook might be the focal point of the room. This undressed window provides warm, natural light and a priceless lookout on nature's changing kaleidoscope of colors.

Within the living room, with its gleaming wood floor and neutral hues, essential furnishings might include a streamlined ivory sofa, a shiny chrome and glass end table, and two ivory contemporary chairs set upon a carpet in neutral or earthy colors. The furnishings face the gorgeous view, perhaps grouped around an antique black Japanese hibachi coffee table, topped with a tall chrome vase filled with orchids, white lilies, or blue irises. For added color, a few modern Japanese prints in ebony frames could be displayed on the white walls. To warm the room's ambience even more, lush plants in shiny black ceramic pots may be scattered throughout the room, mirroring the greenery outside. Lighting fixtures can include several white standing torchères, a chrome tabletop lamp, and recessed accent lights over the artwork. For a softly dramatic effect, an uplight might be placed among several of the plants, casting gentle shadows on one wall and the ceiling. And perhaps a casual grouping of short and tall ivory candles rests upon the hibachi—promising mood lighting after dark.

promote clear thinking, affection, energy, relaxation, or a sense of comfort and calm. For example, tangerine oil is sometimes recommended for calming the spirit, while peppermint oil can be used to inspire alertness.

Other aromatic products that enhance the fragrance of your home include bowls of potpourri or aromatic leaves, scented soaps, perfumed sachets and pillows, atmosphere sprays, bouquets of fresh flowers, and bunches of fresh or dried herbs.

SERENE DECORS: A MINIMALIST LIVING ROOM

Natural and artificial lighting can be orchestrated to create a relaxing, welcoming sanctuary in any room of the home. In a minimalist-style living room, an expansive bay window overlooking a forest and winding

CHAPTER SEVEN

DISCOVERING PARADISE: OUTDOOR LIVING
SPACES AND GENTLE GARDENS

"Almost any garden, if you see it at just the

right moment, can be confused with paradise."

—Henry Mitchell

Millions of us journey to national parks to spend a few days in the pristine wilderness. We're moved by mountain peaks, waterfalls, canyons,

meadows, and majestic animals and birds in their natural habitats. And yet, in our gardens at home, when we notice the first violets awakening

after a long winter, or see the autumn sunshine streaming through the red and gold maple leaves like light through a stained-glass window,

we know that we don't have to travel far to experience the earth's wonders. Outdoor living spaces can renew our spirit and senses every day.

What could be more blissful than lying on a porch hammock, reveling in the promise of a summer's day? Today, porches are enjoying a

well-deserved renaissance because they can stretch a home's living space and enhance its appeal. They are peaceful sanctuaries

where good company and the beauty of the great outdoors can be savored.

Creating Outdoor Living Rooms

In the Victorian era, porches were considered essential extensions of the well-dressed home. They were havens for women's charitable society meetings, gracious teas and dinner parties, and discreet courting under the stars. After World War II, when countless Victorian homes were torn down to make way for modern, low-maintenance houses, the front and back porches, wraparound veranda, and side porch often took a backseat to the popular patio designs of the day. Today, however, the porch is enjoying a renaissance, as people everywhere are discovering that this outdoor room not only adds beauty to their home's facade but helps protect the home from the sun's intense rays, saving on air-conditioning costs. The porch also provides a warm weather living room for entertaining, alfresco dining, reading, and meditating, and it's a superb place from which to watch nature. While some homes have a traditional open-air porch, others have screened porches to keep insects and animals at

LEFT: This courtyard is especially inviting because of its elegant wooden furnishings, warm brick floor, sheltering pergola, and romantic jungle of flowers and greenery. It's a perfect haven for dining outdoors, reading a great mystery, or playing with the family dog.

OPPOSITE: The vibrant spirit of this porch comes from an eclectic medley of casual and ornate garden furnishings, such as the unique rock "vases" and templelike light fixture.

living spaces that can promote hospitality or quiet relaxation include open-air decks, romantic courtyards, sunny patios, loggias (roofed galleries on the sides of homes), and decorative gazebos.

Part of the joy of creating outdoor living rooms is that they can be simply or elaborately furnished and still feel enchanting, for nature is always there to provide dramatic lighting, cooling breezes, and calming fragrance, color, and sound. A wide variety of outdoor furnishings is available, such as classical or ornate cast-iron garden benches, tables, and chairs; colorful Parisian bistro chairs; minimalist metal, teak, and mahogany furnishings; and ancient-looking garden benches crafted from stone. Synthetic wicker is a favorite all-weather material for outdoor rooms of every style. Synthetic mesh hammocks, woven cotton hammocks, and wooden porch swings are also popular. Outdoor furnishings crafted from branches, roots, and twigs are sought after, now that this rustic Victorian-era camp furniture style is back in vogue.

While porch floors can be done in materials such as painted wood planks, granite dimension stone, mottled slate, or terra-cotta or marble

bay. A new favorite is the convertible porch, which can be adjusted to serve as an open, screened, or totally enclosed porch with glazed inserts. Some porches even have elaborate fireplaces, which make cozy focal points for friends to gather around and tell ghost stories at Halloween or enjoy a cup of cheer during the festive winter holiday season. Other delightful outdoor

OPPOSITE: A hot tub can create a tranquil focal point in an outdoor garden room. This custom-built wooden deck equipped with a soothing hot tub and sound system offers an idyllic setting for enjoying the pleasures of pulsing water, gentle music, fragrant flowers, and lovely breezes.

LEFT: A sunlit place to entertain, talk on the phone, or watch children play, this warm wooden deck inspires a feeling of serenity. Its rich wood color, vibrant container gardens, and comfy furnishings blend seamlessly with the surrounding forest.

tiles, open-air courtyards can benefit from a lovely treatment of flagstones, cobblestone or brick walkways, stamped and colored concrete (fashioned to resemble cobblestone, brick, or slate), decorative European stepping-stones, and mosaic tile designs. Container gardens add spirit to any outdoor room and can help create the rustic or romantic, Oriental or ancient mood you long to create. You can choose from decorative cast-stone urns, terra-cotta or colorful ceramic pots, and wooden window-box planters, to name a few. Decorators often suggest that you repeat the colors of your container garden blooms in the fabrics you choose for the cushions, pillows, tablecloths, and other accessories in your outdoor living room. If you fill your porch with pots of blue, white, and yellow

OPPOSITE: Chinese philosopher Lao-tzu believed, "The softest things in the world overcome the hardest things in the world." In this timeless water garden, the mirrorlike surface of a man-made pond inspires thoughts of beauty and peace, offering an antidote to the hectic pace of daily life.

RIGHT: This secret garden has a definite Victorian flair, thanks to its shady, well-tended trees, solid stone walls and walkway, and lovely pond graced with ornaments. The decorative wrought-iron garden chairs and table also add to the sanctuary's genteel ambience.

flowers, try using these hues in your decor for visual flow. Or, if your home is surrounded by a monochromatic garden, you might spotlight this color along with its complementary hue in the fabrics you choose.

Other outdoor accessories that help create an atmosphere of comfort and tranquility include tall acrylic market umbrellas for protection from the afternoon sun; lush green plants perched on pedestals; wrought-iron plant stands filled with container gardens; fountains and statuary; hanging flower baskets overflowing with bright blooms and vines; wind chimes; sisal and tatami floor mats; an array of colorful candles (including tapers, torches, and votives of bug-deterring citronella); baskets of seashells; hummingbird feeders; and binoculars to view wildlife up close.

Creating Your Peaceful Garden

Just as homes can be remembered for their soothing personalities, so can gardens, real and imaginary. If you've read Frances Hodgson Burnett's unforgettable children's book, *The Secret Garden*, or if you've seen the film *Enchanted April*, about four women who find emotional healing in a seaside Italian garden, you know the mystical allure of such flowering rooms. Whether you already have a natural sanctuary outside your back door or long to create one, there are countless garden schemes from which to choose. Popular designs that can help inspire relaxation and renewal include the cottage garden, the Japanese garden, the ornamental garden, and the water garden.

It is said that gardens should harmonize with a landscape's surrounding architecture, so if your home has a contemporary design, a minimalist Japanese garden or a water garden may look fitting. On the other hand, a traditional home can look serene with a formal ornamental garden, while an Arts and Crafts, country, or Victorian home may appear enchanting surrounded by cottage or water gardens. Of course, planning your outdoor landscape is an artistic endeavor that needn't

This lovely arbor and bench create a tranquil garden room for viewing colorful butterflies and birds, and savoring the fragrance of countless roses. It's also a perfect spot for quiet prayer, meditation, or just gazing up at the stars at night.

134

A classic wrought-iron gate opens onto this lush garden, where a rustic birdhouse invites feathered visitors. Though the vibrant lilies are favorite flowers among avid gardeners, the unchecked height of the plants and their casual arrangement makes this peaceful garden feel as if it was designed by nature rather than by human hands.

follow strict guidelines; many gardeners create their own designs according to their terrain, climate, and personal preferences. When designing an outdoor retreat to calm the senses and the soul, it's good to remember that seas of blue and lavender flowers and green plants will suggest peacefulness, while expansive beds of hot red, orange, and yellow blooms will create an electric, energetic mood.

Cottage Gardens Cottage gardens call to mind quaint English thatched homes adorned with tall blue delphiniums, multihued cosmos, and pink hollyhocks. Such picture-perfect spots feature a riot of annuals, perennials, and herbs surrounded by picket fences, garden gates, and often a cobblestone, brick, or gravel pathway that leads up to the home. Wooden pergolas or arbors cascading with red or yellow roses, lavender wisteria, violet clematis, or blue morning glories often grace the entrance and can be used throughout the garden—along with shrubbery and trees—to provide natural walls. Such cottage garden rooms are ideal refuges where you might place ornamental benches, water fountains, or statuary. By dividing your floral landscape into sections, you'll visually expand the space, enabling the garden to be discovered one room at a time.

PEACEFUL PLEASURES

Planting a Butterfly Garden

Poetically referred to as "flying flowers," butterflies add color and joie de vivre to any garden setting. Like birds, their needs for water, food, and shelter can be met easily in the backyard garden. Here are a few hints:

- Pale-hued, neutral, or cool-colored plants that caterpillars seem to prefer include aspens, birches, black cherry, cabbage, clover, cottonwood, dogwood, milkweed, snapdragon, violets, and willows.
- Butterflies are attracted to sunlit masses of flowers that feature single rows of petals, since these are easier to land on than flowers with double rows of petals.
- A few nectar-rich posies that entice butterflies are aster, black-eyed Susan, daisy, foxglove, hollyhocks, iris, lavender, lilac, petunia, phlox, purple coneflower, salvia, sunflower, and thistle. Blue and purple flowers are especially inviting.
- Since birds enjoy feasting on caterpillars and butterflies, try to plant your butterfly gardens away from any nesting boxes, bird feeders, or trees that birds seem to live in.
- Shallow birdbaths, puddles, and water gardens can create alluring drinking spots for butterflies.

Japanese Gardens Japanese gardens radiate mystical beauty, for they are created to harmonize with nature and make onlookers feel at one with the earth, water, and sky. Some are Zen-like, pared down to the most basic elements in order to inspire meditation. A Japanese "dry landscape garden," for example, might feature a courtyard with a symbolic waterfall made of pebbles, surrounded by raked sand or gravel, a few leafy green plants, a small stone lantern, and a single Japanese maple tree. The tea garden is small in scale but has a lush and intricate design that includes an outer garden with a waiting bench and several inner gardens divided by bamboo or dried root fences and gates that encourage visitors to journey away from the cares of the world into the calming realm of nature. The *roji* (path) to the tea house is meant to evoke the feeling of a wild, untamed landscape. It consists of leafy evergreens, velvety moss, and ferns, as well as stepping-stones, lanterns, and water basins for cleansing before entering the tea house.

For anyone who wants to create a Japanese-inspired decorative garden, the key thing to remember is that simplicity and naturalism are the ideal, so ornamentation should be selective. Japanese gardens often include gentle pathways of stepping-stones, bark, timber slices, or gravel that may lead to an outdoor building or a waterfall; a variety of lush green plants, evergreens, azaleas, bamboo, cherry trees, and Japanese maples; weathered stone Buddhas and lanterns; a tall stupa, or stone tower, which is often used to create a feeling of distance; small ponds and waterfalls; decorative stone

or wooden bridges arching over water or a dry garden; and, always, a sense of balance and asymmetry, with decorative elements united in groupings of odd numbers, such as three rocks, five shrubs, or seven evergreen trees.

Ornamental Gardens   Ornamental gardens are enhanced not only by formal or naturalistic floral schemes, but by the presence of lovely statuary or urns, stone lanterns, birdbaths, fountains, arbors, arches, garden follies, and garden gates that serve as focal points. Statues might be of timeless classical, mythical, religious, or Oriental beings, or of whimsical animals in more casual settings. A formal geometric garden with well-tended beds of flowers and carefully trimmed hedges should be accented with a few key dramatic ornaments to capture the eye and provide a sense of permanence and structure. During the Victorian era, ornaments were widely used in the kitchen, herb, and formal rose gardens. Favorite Victorian garden art included sundials, armillaries (horological spheres), and classic Italian-style statues, stone pots, and benches cast in lead. Today's ornamental garden rooms can be ideal spots for rejuvenation. Place an altar across from a garden bench

139

PEACEFUL PLEASURES

Attracting Guests to Your Outdoor Sanctuaries

Part of the joy of bird-watching at home is seeing your favorite songbirds return to your gardens year after year. Here are a few tips for attracting birds through all four seasons:

- While many birds prefer seeds, some are primarily insect eaters (warblers, kinglets, woodpeckers), and others prefer fruit (bluebirds, robins, waxwings). Hummingbirds feast on both insects and nectar. Birding books can acquaint you with the best food and feeder choices for your locale, and help you decide whether to provide food only in the winter or all year round.

- Since bacteria grow readily in feeders, be sure to keep yours clean.

- Place feeders away from flower beds because scattered seeds may foster weeds.

- Trees that attract insects—such as coniferous trees—and those that provide berries or fruits can be ideal food sources.

- Birds are drawn to moving water, so consider installing a birdbath that recirculates dripping water, or a small fountain or a garden pond with a waterfall.

- Avoid using chemicals in your yard. They can poison beneficial insects and harm birds, butterflies, and other wildlife, and they may pose a danger to pets.

A wide variety of ornaments can add character and a sense of permanence to your garden, such as classic urns, fountains, statues, armillary spheres, sundials, and Victorian gazing globes. This spirited ornamental fountain glistens with color and pattern, and enchants with the soothing sounds of moving water.

Legendary British gardener Gertrude Jekyll was also an artist, who compared her more than three hundred garden masterpieces to colorful Impressionist paintings. Jekyll said, "The love of gardening is a seed that, once sown, never dies." This lush ornamental garden attests to its owners' enduring devotion to the art of horticulture.

garden can be as simple as installing a decorative birdbath or water trough. Or, if you long for a more elaborate Garden of Eden right in your backyard, you can purchase a prefabricated pond or even an artificial waterfall from various companies. Ponds made of fiberglass or polyethylene plastic can be found in a wide range of sizes. Flexible pond liners made of UV-resistant rubber are also available. Garden suppliers offer electric pumps and filters that help keep pond water clear, but a number of submerged plants can help reduce algae naturally. A variety of aquatic plants can often be grown in such havens, including water lilies and cardinal flowers. The vivid orange and silvery white bodies of koi—a type of carp bred specifically for ornamental ponds—lend beautiful spots of color to a gentle green sanctuary. Water gardens also attract a wonderful variety of wild creatures, including birds, turtles, frogs, salamanders, dragonflies, butterflies, water striders, raccoons, foxes, rabbits, and squirrels.

under a sheltering canopy of trees to fashion a serene meditation spot for yourself that's far from the workday world. Or link two garden rooms with arbors of roses and a path of stepping-stones set amidst ferns and stone statues of garden fairies to create a magical world for yourself and your children.

Water Gardens   Water gardens are a wonderful antidote to stress, as well as an ideal way to create a refuge for wildlife. The Chinese believe that a garden without water cannot have good feng shui, and that birdbaths, ponds, waterfalls, and fountains attract chi. Creating your water

SELECTED BIBLIOGRAPHY

Ackerman, Diane. *A Natural History of the Senses*. New York: Random House, 1990.

Breuilly, Elizabeth, Joanne O'Brien, and Martin Palmer. *Religions of the World*. New York: Facts on File, 1997.

Brussat, Frederic, and Mary Ann Brussat. *Spiritual Literacy: Reading the Sacred in Everyday Life*. New York: Scribner, 1996.

Flanders, Angela. *Aromatics*. New York: Clarkson N. Potter, 1995.

Gawler, Ian. *Peace of Mind*. New York: Avery Publishing Group, 1989.

Lawlor, Anthony. *The Temple in the House: Finding the Sacred in Everyday Architecture*. New York: G. P. Putnam's Sons, 1994.

McConnell, Malcolm. "Faith Can Help You Heal," *Reader's Digest*, October 1998.

Michaud, Ellen. "It's the Little Things . . . That Drive You Crazy," *Prevention*, July 1998.

Ornstein, Robert, and David Sobel. *Healthy Pleasures*. Reading, Mass.: Addison Wesley Publishing Company, 1989.

Rybczynski, Witold. *Home: A Short History of an Idea*. New York: Penguin Books, 1986.

Streep, Peg. *Altars Made Easy*. San Francisco: HarperCollins, 1997.

Thompson, Angel. *Feng Shui: How to Achieve the Most Harmonious Arrangement of Your Home and Office*. New York: St. Martin's Griffin, 1996.

Walters, Anna Lee. *The Spirit of Native America*. San Francisco: Chronicle Books, 1989.

PHOTOGRAPHY CREDITS

Index

Accessories, 97–106
  outdoor, 131–133
  personalized, 70
  scouting for, 91
Air purification, 120
Altar(s)
  creating, 102–106
  history of, 101
Arts and Crafts, 27–28
  dining room, 26
  entry hall, 74
  furnishings, 88, 91
  living rooms, 11, 74,
    74–75

Balance, 14–15, 25
Baldwin, Billy, 35, 79
Bathroom(s), 95
  accessories, 99
  cool-hued, 94
  eclectic, 83
  understated, 57
  warm-hued, 115
Bed(s), 87, 92, 93
Bedroom(s), 86
  blue and white, 96
  cottage, 21, 56, 91–93
  eclectic, 29, 90
  guest, 69

home office in, 109
Japanese style, 15
  neutral-hued, 55, 71, 72,
    114
  Zen-like, 32–33
Bird watching, 140
Black color, 50
Blue color, 40, 52, 56, 96
Butterfly garden, 137

Candles, 115, 118, 123
Chi (cosmic energy), 14–15
Chinese homes, 13–14
Clutter-free spaces, 33
Color(s), 41–61
  combinations of, 45–47
  complementary, 43
  cool, 50–55, 52, 56–57
  lighting and, 43–45
  neutral, 46, 47–50, 51
  tips on, 49
  and visual weight, 22
  warm, 58, 59, 60
Cottage style, 28
  bedrooms, 21, 56, 91–93
  gardens, 137
Courtyard, 128
Cream color, 50

Deck(s), 130, 131
Design, 19–39
  planning, 20–21
Dining room(s)
  Arts and Crafts, 26
  eclectic, 36
  Japanese style, 25, 106
  with natural light, 12
  nature-inspired, 66, 82
  warm-hued, 58, 59
  with water garden, 119

Eclectic style, 28–35
  bathroom, 83
  bedroom, 29, 90
  dining room, 37
  home office, 108
  living rooms, 42, 52–53,
    124
  outdoor spaces, 129
Entry hall, 118
  Arts and Crafts, 74

Fabrics, 89–91
  natural, 71
Family room(s)
  contrasting textures, 64
  Southwestern style, 61
Feng shui, 13–14, 84–85

Floor(s), 67–68
  outdoor, 129–131
  stone, 37, 69
Fragrance, 122–125
Furnishings, 79–82
  natural, 68
  outdoor, 129
  selecting, 84–91

Garden(s), 134–141
  butterfly, 137
  container, 131–133
  cottage, 137
  Japanese, 119, 138–139
  ornamental, 139–141
  Victorian, 133, 139
  water, 14, 119, 132, 138,
    139, 141
Gothic style
  bed, 92
  living room, 102
Gray color, 50
Green color, 52

Hibachis, 25, 35
Home office(s)
  bedroom corner, 109
  casual, 43, 108
  eclectic, 109

Hot tub, outdoor, *130*

Interior landscape, 19

Japanese style, 13, 35
  bedroom, *15*
  dining rooms, 25, *106,*
    119
  gardens, *119*, 138–139
  living rooms, *23, 24,* 25,
    34

Kitchen(s)
  contrasting textures, *62*
  decorating tips, 54
  eclectic, *65*
  nature-inspired, *17*
  neutral-hued, *20*
  Southwestern, 61
  warm-hued, 58

Lighting, 112–115
  and color, 43–45
  natural, *12, 113–116*
  and visual weight, 22
Living room(s)
  Arts and Crafts, *11,* 74,
    74–75
  brightly colored, *44*
  cozy, *10, 80*
  eclectic, *42, 52–53, 124*
  elegant, *8, 22, 45, 81*
  Gothic style, *102*
  Japanese style, *23, 24,* 25

minimalist, *84–85,* 125
nature-inspired, *18*
neutral-hued, *8, 46, 47,*
  51, 76–77, 125
outdoor, 128–133
Southwestern, *48–49, 60*

Meditation, 107
Mies van der Rohe,
  Ludwig, 27
Minimalist style, 35
  living room, *84–85,* 125
Modular wall system, 39
Morris, William, 27, 28, 73
Music, 121

Native American homes, 13
Nature
  decorations, 77
  products, 67–71
  restorative powers of,
    63–64
Noise control, 117

Orange color, *40,* 58, *84*
Ornamental garden(s),
  139–141, *140, 141*
Outdoor living spaces,
  127–141. *See also*
  Garden(s)

Paints, natural, 68, 76–77
Paneling, natural, 68
Partitions, 35, 38–39

Pattern, 66
Plants
  air purifying, 120
  butterfly garden, 137
Porch(es), *126,* 128–133
  eclectic, *129*
Private sanctuaries, *30,*
  36–39
Proportion, 21–25

Radial balance, 25
Red color, 58
Rybczynski, Witold, 11, 82

Schweitzer, Albert, 17
Screens, 35, 38–39
Shade, 43
Shoji, 35
Single-family houses, 12
Small rooms, decorating, 39
Sound, 121–122
  noise control, 117
Southwestern style, 36
  family room, 61
  kitchen, 61
  living rooms, *48–49, 60*
Storage ideas, 33
Sunrooms, *30, 31, 113*
Symmetry, 25

Television, 16
Texture(s), 64–66
  contrasting, *20, 62*
Tint, 43

Twain, Mark, 9, 10
  house of, 10–11

Victorian garden, *133,* 139
Violet color, 55
Visual weight, 22

Wallpaper, 73, *73*
Water garden(s), *14, 132,*
  139, 141
  Japanese, *119, 138*
White color, 50
Wind chimes, *121, 122*
Window seat(s), *29,* 36, *99*
Wright, Frank Lloyd, 81

Yellow color, 58
Yin and yang, 14–15